Developing and Applying Assessments i
hands-on guide full of important informati
use assessment as a process for improving st
This must-read book pragmatically demonstrates the connection of assessment
to curricular goals, program goals, and planned student outcomes by skillfully
guiding the reader through all aspects of assessment, including the often-daunting
practice of creating meaningful, functional, and efficient music assessments that
result in improved music learning for students. This book encourages assessment
literacy and skill building to support career-long interest in understanding how
students learn, what they learn, and how best to teach them.
    – **Ann C. Clements,** *Director, Center for Pedagogy in Arts and Design,*
                                        The Pennsylvania State University

There is a void in the literature for music teacher educators who help undergraduate
music education students examine how and why assessment is used in music
classrooms. This workbook-style text – with learning experiences, worksheets,
and activities – certainly helps fill that void. This book is scholarly, practical, and
easy-to-read – a must for collegiate music methods classes.
    – **Glenn E. Nierman,** *Past President, National Association*
                                        for Music Education

Developing and Applying Assessments in the Music Classroom is a great resource
for developing assessments for specific learning targets, equipping future educators
with the tools they need to inspire their students to reach their best potential.
    – **Denese Odegaard,** *President, National Association for*
                                        Music Education

The learning experiences contained here – each stemming from actual practice and
supported by years of research – will allow future and current music educators to
develop proficiencies that will be applicable on their first day of teaching and
throughout their careers. Parkes and Burrack have carefully delineated the best means
to assess each of the inherent facets of music learning: the products of student learning;
the processes by which they learned; the programs that are designed to help them
learn; and the best practices of the educators who support their learning. *Developing
and Applying Assessments in the Music Classroom* will transform the work of music
educators and, more importantly, support the vibrant music-learning community that
engages teachers and learners in the amazing experiences only music can provide.
    – **Douglas C. Orzolek,** *Director of Graduate Programs*
                                        in Music Education, University of St. Thomas

With *Developing and Applying Assessments in the Music Classroom*, the editors
and authors contribute a valuable resource for future and current music educators
at all levels. Through discussions of general principles and music-specific examples,
readers will appreciate this book as a companion and guide through the often-
confusing landscape of measurement, evaluation, and testing as it is encountered in
the teaching of the musical art. It will be equally valuable to individual teachers in
their own classroom contexts as it is for administrative leaders of music programs
and program-wide teams designing and aligning music curricula. By approaching
assessment of musical learning through the perspectives presented in this volume,
as music educators we can increase the effectiveness, impact, and authenticity of
our educational practice – to the ultimate benefit of our students.
    – **Bret P. Smith,** *Associate Professor of Music Education,*
                                        Central Washington University

Developing and Applying Assessments in the Music Classroom

Developing and Applying Assessments in the Music Classroom addresses the challenges faced by today's K-12 educators and future music educators who are expected to utilize and incorporate assessment data as a hallmark of student learning and reflection of effective teaching. Highlighting best practices while presenting current scholarship and literature, this practical workbook-style text provides future music teachers with a framework for integrating assessment processes in the face of a certain lack of understanding and possible dissatisfaction with assessment tools and tasks. Each chapter is prefaced by an overview outlining learning expectations and essential questions and supplemented throughout by an array of pedagogical features:

- Discussion prompts
- Activities and worksheets
- Learning experiences
- Expanded reference lists

Citing examples across a range of musical settings – e.g., band, chorus, orchestra, jazz, and piano and guitar labs – *Developing and Applying Assessments in the Music Classroom* builds from the classroom assessment paradigm, encouraging teachers to create assessment tasks most appropriate to their curricula goals and planned student outcomes. Joined by fellow experts in the field Brian C. Wesolowski and Phillip Payne, the authors invite readers to explore and apply the material in authentic ways to inspire student learning through a comprehensive approach to educative assessment.

Kelly A. Parkes is Director and Associate Professor of the Music and Music Education program at Teachers College, Columbia University.

Frederick Burrack is Director of Assessment, Professor of Music Education, Graduate Chair for Music, and Distinguished Graduate Faculty at Kansas State University.

Developing and Applying Assessments in the Music Classroom

Kelly A. Parkes and
Frederick Burrack

Routledge
Taylor & Francis Group

NEW YORK AND LONDON

First published 2020
by Routledge
52 Vanderbilt Avenue, New York, NY 10017

and by Routledge
2 Park Square, Milton Park, Abingdon, Oxon, OX14 4RN

Routledge is an imprint of the Taylor & Francis Group, an informa business

Library of Congress Cataloging-in-Publication Data
A catalog record for this book has been requested

ISBN: 978-0-367-19421-5 (hbk)
ISBN: 978-0-367-19422-2 (pbk)
ISBN: 978-0-429-20230-8 (ebk)

Typeset in Sabon
by Apex CoVantage, LLC

Contents

Foreword

Individual assessment was established in music long before Bach auditioned for positions as a church organist. Group assessment in the US occurred in the first few decades of the 20th century with vigorous solo and ensemble contests. At about the same time, psychologists began to wonder whether aptitude in music was anything like IQ tests. Perhaps due to the large influx of students following World War II, college deans became interested in assessment as an entrance requirement for music majors. James Aliferis published an entrance examination (based primarily on music theory skills) that was endorsed by the National Association of Schools of Music. As a fledging public school music teacher at the time, it occurred to me that a college entrance examination and a high school graduation examination for talented students were one and the same; thus began a career-long interest in assessment in music. In the following decade or two there was a flurry of textbooks describing the content of old and new music tests. None of these tests at any level made a significant impact upon the profession and were little used, the primary reason being that music teachers did not know how to administer the tests and little or no idea on how to interpret the results. This book, by experienced specialists, is unique in that it has as its focus the music educator and assessment, preschool through college. The book takes the reader from the establishment of program objectives to their application in the classroom. It is further remarkable in being scaled for use in extant music education methods courses. This means that students will quickly learn the applicability of assessment ideas to their teaching. Despite the rhetoric on arts assessment, the music educator is truly alone. Coursework in assessment given by a college of education or department of psychology seldom applies to teaching and learning in music. School administrators and school board members assume that music is valued and the content rigorous, as statements as early as 1927 by school administrators and later by the National Education Association argue for a "well-balanced school curriculum in which music and the like is to be included with other important subjects such as mathematics, history, and science." This support has not translated well in practice. In 1980, John Goodlad reported a strong thread of pessimism among arts educators regarding present and potential support for arts education in the schools. Music, alone, is valued for its sociopolitical goals of education and schooling, but the strength of attaining these goals and others is unknown, requiring a fresh look at assessment. An inspection of the curricular programs of visual arts, dance, and theatre portrays significant differences in their priorities, and there is no documentation of changes in music program objectives to accommodate STEAM or the priorities of process and product. The idea of progress does not hold in the same way as in other subjects. A jazz or rock concert is no more complicated than a performance of Renaissance music. Music performing groups seldom select music in a second year that could demonstrate "annual yearly progress," an almost infeasible task. The teacher is also responsible for individual and small-group goals (the concert mistress and even the trombones (?) are expected to progress). If the music program is focused on ensembles of iPads or improvising various sounds such as in Musical Futures, we know that it is possible to approach any art form naively without any prior conceptions or knowledge of techniques employed and that assessment is even more necessary to avoid the acceptance of curricular issues as experienced by Ronald B. Thomas in the clever Manhattanville Music Curriculum. Our assessment practices will be compared with those used in Next Generation Science Standards.

The book was not written as a response to the relentless critiques of the nation's public schools; its purpose is to enable the music educator to formulate valid and fair tasks and to interpret the results in terms of the student's and the school's culture. The authors clearly emphasize the importance of culture, philosophy, and taxonomies in formulating priority objectives that are attainable and measurable. I sense that the user of the materials in this book has the potential to be an instructional leader in music education. This leadership is extremely important in that education itself is searching for leaders and few school administrators are competent to judge valid school music programs. Best practices come from an ability to analyze data and know when data have been interpreted incorrectly, have been manipulated, or are simply false. Only with valid data can a teacher know whether his or her program is rigorous and focusing on values, values that are the basis for teaching objectives in music. Sponsored and collegiate research has traditionally been on small units of music education, not on improving music education programs. That fact, alone, is reason to read this text from cover to cover and become familiar with employing the musical and educational constructs of the profession.

Richard Colwell, Professor Emeritus
University of Illinois

Preface

Assessment. This word typically conjures images of tests, feelings of anxiety, and a sense of impending judgment. Public perception of assessment typically centers around either standardized tests or accountability and neither are particularly inviting. The perception of assessment is typically negative. Many, if not most, individuals have had poor experiences with assessment in their own education in K-12 schooling or in higher education. Music educators are not immune to this, and in response to an ongoing need for K-12 teachers to be skilled in generating and using assessment data as part of highly effective teaching, we conceived the idea for this book. We have already published a book detailing a series of assessment tasks and research tools for K-12 teachers (Burrack & Parkes, 2018), yet some research (e.g., Beason, 2017) indicates that K-12 teachers are not aware of the published assessment tasks, nor do they know how to use them. It seems that our higher education colleagues are also, in some instances, not aware there are useful assessment tools that college students could be learning about and utilizing in their coursework/field experiences as they prepare to enter the field.

There is a problem in our profession with what we call "assessment literacy," and it is perhaps noticeable in higher education faculty at large. Our concern is with those professors teaching in music teacher education programs within universities. Recent research findings (Parkes & Rawlings, 2019) show that some college music education professors report learning about assessment on the job while they were K-12 teachers and others report taking a course more often in graduate school rather than in undergraduate studies; notwithstanding these experiences, many described a certain lack of understanding and highlighted a general dissatisfaction with assessment; and, of more concern, there was little evidence of pedagogical content knowledge used in teaching assessment strategies.

The goal of this book is to provide educative information about assessment to undergraduate music education students in a workbook with relevant research along with learning experiences, worksheets, and activities. Music teacher educators are responsible for preparing future teachers how to use assessments in K-12 classrooms, yet a series of studies (e.g., LaCognata, 2013; McQuarrie & Sherwin, 2013; Orzolek, 2016; Russell & Austin, 2010) indicate that K-12 music teachers are underprepared to use assessment in their classrooms. Our aim is to provide a text for college music education professors to use within an existing course to educate future K-12 teachers about assessment. We hope this book will serve the need to educate undergraduate music education students about assessment in an approachable manner without adding the need for additional coursework. This book, or selected chapters within, may be used alongside other books in methods courses, practicum experiences, and fieldwork. In providing focused information and activities to develop assessment literacy and skill in undergraduate music education students, we hope to contribute to the education of future music teachers.

The contents of this book are very different to traditional assessment texts that typically deal with classical test theory and test construction. Our book builds from the classroom assessment paradigm: we suggest teachers should create assessment tasks to be used in their instruction that are most appropriate to their curricula goals, their program goals, and their planned student outcomes. We have nine chapters presenting a series of foci, each dealing with different areas of assessment appropriate for K-12 music settings, written in a way that first educates the reader with current scholarship, literature, examples, and information. Each chapter then provides a series of discussion prompts, experiences, or activities and, in some appropriate chapters, assignments for readers to apply the content.

Chapter 1 (Parkes) describes educational assessment and the historical developments that led to an increased focus on assessment in music classrooms. Topics of the chapter include traditional approaches, modern approaches, standardized music tests, classroom assessments, model cornerstone assessments, and technology.

Chapter 2 (Burrack & Parkes) explains the importance of assessment in schools and describes the purpose of assessment as educative. Topics included are assessment processes, recent developments in learning outcomes, the notion of evaluation as part of assessment, and overarching assessment principles.

Chapter 3 (Burrack & Parkes) addresses the rationale for why formal assessment is needed in music programs. The chapter provides a framework for integrating assessment process into music programs. Topics include developing overarching goals, program and course learning outcomes, and detailed instructions for writing outcomes. The alignment of goals and outcomes is underscored and establishing a culture of assessment is recommended

Chapter 4 (Wesolowski & Payne) describes the processes by which music educators can develop student-learning outcomes, align assessment tasks with stated outcomes, and create scoring devices to collect data in order to provide detailed, timely, and meaningful feedback and analysis for both students and educators. Topics of the chapter include a review of common educational taxonomies and related frameworks, crafting learning objectives, preplanning assessment processes, developing assessment blueprints and tables of specifications, defining learning outcomes, and selecting appropriate item-types.

Chapter 5 (Wesolowski) addresses the evaluation of music classroom testing quality using three key indicators: validity, reliability, and fairness. Topics of the chapter include defining tests, latent constructs, and inferences; traditional (i.e., large-scale testing) perspectives of validity, reliability, and fairness; and new music classroom perspectives of validity, reliability, and fairness. The new framework for conceptualizing validity, reliability, and fairness in classroom music contexts provides a more accessible, qualitative approach for teachers to reflect upon the quality of their classroom music assessments.

Chapter 6 (Parkes) describes performance assessments and their use in music classrooms. The definitions of direct, authentic, and alternative assessments will be given, and processes for developing performance assessment tasks and scoring devices will be outlined. Topics include developing criteria, performance domains, and the use of performance assessments including portfolios.

Chapter 7 (Burrack & Payne) details strategies to help better understand future students' experience in and throughout a music program. Indirect assessment processes also can expose students' self-concept as a musician and learner of music and beliefs in students' ability to succeed as a musician (musical self-efficacy and musician role identity). These approaches, while often not considered as learning assessment, could be useful to a music teacher to provide proper and effective documentation. Techniques are provided to analyze and compare findings to direct assessments revealing learning influences that can guide instructional and curricular decisions.

Chapter 8 (Wesolowski) describes and analyzes classroom testing data with the intent of informing future teaching and learning processes and improving future test uses from both a class-centered perspective and an individual student-centered perspective. Concepts covered include item- and person-ordering, item difficulty, person ability, item- and person-discrimination, and distractor analyses.

Chapter 9 (Payne & Burrack) addresses the issue of using assessment to enhance program development. Assessment data are collected to guide music teachers toward decisions regarding curriculum, structure, staffing, and student learning through a comprehensive program assessment plan. We have also included a glossary of terms used within the book.

This book has several features that both professors and students may find helpful. Each chapter sets out learning expectations and essential questions at the front, and students will find these useful in developing their study notes for each chapter. There are *Learning Experiences* placed at certain points in the text that should be completed during the reading. This will allow students to engage with the topic being described and usually these activities are experiential in nature. Activity worksheets are also included at salient points in each chapter to allow students to have hands-on engagement with the knowledge they are acquiring through the text.

Our prime audience for this workbook is college undergraduate music education students and other student professionals completing study to further meet teaching license/certification levels, who want to use assessment as a process for improving student learning and their own teaching. Assessment is simply one part in the cycle of good teaching and learning, and we hope our readers will enjoy learning a new approach to assessment.

Kelly A. Parkes

References

Beason, C. (2017). *A mixed methods design study investigating the use of a music authentic performance assessment tool by high school band directors to measure student musical growth* (Unpublished doctoral dissertation). Texas Wesleyan University, Fort Worth.

Burrack, F., & Parkes, K. A. (Eds.). (2018). *Applying Model Cornerstone Assessments in K – 12 music: A research-supported approach.* Lanham, MD: Rowman & Littlefield.

LaCognata, J. (2013). Current student assessment practices of high school band directors in the United States. In T. Brophy (Ed.), *Music assessment across cultures and continents* (pp. 109–128). Chicago, IL: GIA Publications.

McQuarrie, S., & Sherwin, R. (2013). Assessment in music education: Relationships between training, experience, and common practice. In T. Brophy (Ed.), *Music assessment across cultures and continents* (pp. 141–152). Chicago, IL: GIA Publications.

Orzolek, D. (2016). In their own words: Music teachers' beliefs about assessment. In T. S. Brophy, J. Marlatt, & G. K. Ritcher (Eds.), *Connecting practice, measurement, and evaluation: Selected papers from the 5th international symposium on assessment in music education* (pp. 447–454). Chicago, IL: GIA Publications.

Parkes, K. A., & Rawlings, J. R. (2019). The preparation of music teacher educators to use and teach assessment. *Contributions to Music Education, 45,* 145–165.

Russell, J. A., & Austin, J. R. (2010). Assessment practices of secondary music teachers. *Journal of Research in Music Education, 58,* 37–54. doi:10.1177/0022429409360062

Acknowledgments

We would like to thank Phillip Payne and Brian C. Wesolowski most especially. Without their support, collegiality, wisdom, patience, and hard work, this book simply would not have been written. Not only are they strong musicians and music educators in their own right, they considerably improved the contents of this book with their thoughtful suggestions and powerful contributions. We deeply appreciate their counsel and friendship. We are proud to have them in this book and to count them as our most respected colleagues.

1 Historical Foundations

Kelly A. Parkes

Chapter Overview

This chapter explores the political policies and educational developments that led to an increased focus on assessment in music classrooms in the USA. The chapter explains traditional and modern assessments, with a focus on classroom assessments.

Learning Expectations for the Chapter

- Describe the political policies that led to modern assessment in music education.
- Describe the difference between traditional and modern assessment measures.
- Identify the difference between standardized and classroom assessments.
- Describe existing measures of music achievement.

Essential Questions for the Chapter

- What are the differences between traditional and modern assessments?
- What are standardized tests?
- What are classroom assessments?
- How are classroom assessments used as part of educational assessment in music?

Introduction

When we consider *assessment* at large, it is important to have clarity around the term. Assessment, as explored in this book, is to be considered as **educational assessment**. Assessment in education is a *process* that includes **measurement** and **evaluation**. The assessment process involves collecting information (data) via a variety of measurement methods that are relevant to making educational decisions. The educational assessment process communicates information about teaching processes and about student learning. This impacts teachers' instructional choices and guides student progress. Measures can be tests, portfolios, checklists, and rubrics. Evaluation occurs when teachers analyze qualitative (words) and quantitative (numerical) data to make a decision of value, worth, merit, or effectiveness. An evaluation is what occurs as a result of an effective assessment process. Evaluations are based on information that has been collected and synthesized to make an educational decision about the extent to which objectives have been achieved. In contrast to evaluations seen on social media platforms (for example, those that determine the quality of restaurants), educational assessments require a wide variety of data and objective measures to guide decisions. Historically, in the USA, learning theories, political decisions, and curriculum reform have impacted educational assessment. Educational assessment is the method by which all aspects of education are measured.

National assessment in the USA started in the late 1960s with the National Assessment of Educational Progress (NAEP, 2016), which included music beginning in the academic year 1971–1972. The NAEP music test includes multiple choice and constructed-response items to illustrate what a nationally representative set of eighth graders know about music. NAEP results represent academic achievement of the nation as a whole. The music portion report (NAEP, 2016) showed that 63% of eighth graders took a music class and that their scores remained similar to the scores of eighth graders who took the test in 2008. These national data suggest that females scored higher on average than their male peers and that students in private schools scored higher on average than those in public schools in music. Although there is a use for large-scale tests, the few that are available in music do not measure achievement of applied music skills or how students apply the knowledge they have attained.

Traditional Approaches

Early approaches to educational assessment were based on objective tests, aligned with behaviorist theories of teaching and learning. Payne (2003) explains that traditional measures were focused on lower-level objectives and structured in a fixed-response style to be machine-scoreable. Early testing would detect correct or incorrect answers on a test by counting the small circles filled in by test takers using Scantron technology. Scantron technology emerged in the 1970s and uses optical mark recognition, identifying dark marks on paper as contrasted by light passing through. Scantron technology is still in use today. These test measures (multiple-choice tests) had evidence of high reliability and were low in cost to administer but also provoked anxiety in students when used for consequential, high-stakes decisions. These measures are what we refer to as standardized tests, developed out of the psychology field's intelligence testing, where they were adapted to measure classroom content. The origin of this format was introduced in education early in the 20th century to measure student achievement but then quickly expanded to be used to modify curricula and pedagogy. In addition to this, achievement data were also used as screenings for military positions, employment in business firms, and entrance to universities. Student-centered teachers opposed the use of such tests from their inception; however, their use persisted as test developers purported their use to identify teacher competence as well as student learning. The tests did not actually reveal information about teacher competence, yet the notion incorrectly persists today. In the public view, these tests were initially supported because they promised educational accountability, and this has since been cultivated politically as evidence of quality in education (Giordano, 2005). Although mostly outside of music, these standardized tests remain prevalent because they provide a "systematic sample of performance obtained under prescribed conditions, scored to definite rules, and capable of evaluation by reference to normative information" (Payne, 2003, p. 578). They are administered across schools, districts, and states to compare students' performance on the test to other students taking the same test. This is called **norm-referenced** testing. When teachers want to determine whether a student has achieved a particular set of knowledge or a specific skill, within a specific discipline, they would use **criterion-referenced** tests that measure specific criteria related to instructional objectives. In this case, scores of other students are not examined and the results of criterion-referenced tests are usually given as percentages.

Traditional approaches to assessment have revolved largely around multiple-choice and essay formats. When used for numeracy and knowledge attainment, this is reasonable. An essay demonstrates literacy of written communication skills, and multiple-choice tests allow test takers to choose the correct answer to a mathematical problem or demonstrate knowledge retention. When we consider educational outcomes for musicality in performance and decision-making in preparation and the creative processes often expected in music learning, modern approaches offer more appropriate assessment methods. In music, there are defined competencies that result in musical behaviors. For example, (a) accurate reading of printed music allows students to reproduce music in performance or (b) recognizing tonality helps maintain melodic flow in improvisation. We can't identify music reading competency until we hear the outcome during a music performance or, in the case of the second example, recognize understanding of tonality until we hear their melodic improvisation. With numerous competencies being part of music learning, modern music assessment processes are essential.

Modern Approaches

There is evidence indicating that public attitudes toward traditional standardized testing are changing as we see the opt-out movement rising in some states in the USA, in which parents are protesting the ways in which schools assess their children. Pizmony-Levy (2018) reported that 11 states had opt-out rates higher than 5%. New York has seen a 20% opt-out rate from annual tests, Colorado 8% for seventh grade and 11% for eighth grade, and Alaska's opt-out rate is 8.5%. This change in attitude toward standardized testing may come from skepticism about the usefulness of standardized tests as well as the desire for education reform. Educational assessment processes and measures have been developed and improved over the past century due to new theories of learning, curricula reform, and political decisions. Policy decisions such as the Elementary and Secondary Education Act of 1965, the changes made to it in 1994, the No Child Left Behind Act in 2001, and the Every Student Succeeds Act in 2015 have increased the focus on student test scores and the evaluation of teachers and, as such, have impacted how assessment is used in US schools.

Modern assessment processes include classroom-embedded exams, authentic assessments, performance assessments, direct and indirect assessments, and portfolio assessments. Modern measures focus on indicators of learning outcomes to better understand how students understand and apply what has been taught. The purpose of an assessment process is to produce data that can be used to improve learning and guide instructional and curricular improvement. Modern assessment processes focus on objectives that require students to interact with content at a high level of complexity. These processes require of a variety of measures exhibiting student-constructed responses that include oral, written, product-based, and observation formats through which students demonstrate learning. Modern assessment processes can be complex and multidimensional (Payne, 2003), with a high level of validity and high evidence of reliability when developers and scorers are trained. Modern assessments can be less threatening to learners and result in information useful to teachers and their students (Payne, 2003). They take into account cognitive and constructivist understandings of learning, research findings that have resulted from multiple educational studies. Modern assessments are cost-effective measures since most are administered in classrooms. Most importantly, the data can be formatively used to support student learning in the music classroom. These assessments enable teachers to engage with students in classroom activities that combine learning and application, thus constructing knowledge together. The learner gains insight about their progress and the teacher receives guidance on how to plan further instruction to meet the learners' needs. These measures allow teachers to be responsive to learners' needs and, when used alongside of standardized tests, can give a comprehensive illustration of learners' knowledge and skills.

Standardized Music Tests

Teachers in music have been required to collect student learning data since 2009, after policies were put in place to increase teacher accountability. In 2009 the American Recovery and Reinvestment Act was enacted and provided over $4 billion to assist educators in meeting the goals of the act. The Race to the Top program (US Department of Education, 2009) was competitive grant funding that rewarded states for developments in reforming education and required some form of accountability. One focus was on developing data systems that measured student growth, ostensibly to also illustrate strengths and weaknesses in teachers. Accountability for K-12 achievement evolved into evaluation systems to illustrate teacher quality by using students' achievement scores. State departments of education required school districts to use large-scale, standardized test data collected in math and reading as evidence of teacher quality. Music teachers (along with other non-tested subject teachers, e.g., physical education) were unable to illustrate their teaching quality because they could not show what their students had learned with data (for a detailed description, see Sherwin & McQuarrie, 2019). Some music teachers were actually evaluated with the math and reading scores of their students, which was a critical misuse of the data. At that time, around 2010, no large-scale music tests existed; however, some of the US states that received Race to the Top funding set about creating them.

A variety of approaches can be seen during the early 21st century in developing large-scale music testing systems as part of evaluating teaching, yet none of them utilized the work of Stufflebeam's (2000) CIPP (Context, Input, Process, and Product) evaluation model to determine quality evaluation systems themselves. This model evaluates educational quality in schools and shows high potential for the evaluation of music teacher evaluation systems (Orzolek, 2019). Research conducted in the early 21st century instead focused on creating measures of music achievement (standardized tests) that would be used, in varying degrees, in teachers' evaluations. Kelly, Cummings, and Gordon (2019) described the Florida Performing Fine Arts Assessment Project that was designed to measure both prepared and on-demand performance tasks, as well as a bank of more traditionally structured test items. Swanson and Shepherd (2019) explained Kentucky's approach, which developed a music listening test that allowed for an authentic application of music knowledge and understanding. Joseph (2019) reported that over five years, Washington state proposed both formative and summative designs to assess music outcomes because formative assessment informs both students and teachers through feedback while shaping instruction, whereas summative assessments determine the summed quality of goal achievement at the end of a period of instruction. Music educators in Texas (Henry, 2019) created a statewide music test that included both knowledge-based and performance-based sections to meet the needs for a standards-based assessment of music. Similarly, in Colorado, Hudson and Gates (2019) explained a partnership between music educators and the Department of Education in Colorado allowing music to be accepted as a core academic subject. This perhaps moved the discipline of music in schools to focus on standards-based assessments, although the underlying purpose was clearly connected to teacher evaluation. In Michigan, (Shaw & Taggart, 2019) assessments were designed to be used by teachers to assess music outcomes resulting in data that could also be used as part of evidence in music teacher evaluations. In South Carolina, Lewis, Burgess, and Fan (2019) described a partnership among the state Department of Education, higher education, and arts educators that allowed for the creation of multiple-choice and performance tasks as part of a state-level arts assessment program.

Learning Experience: With a class partner or group, review some of the literature referenced in this section and other scholarship you can find on music assessments in schools, then discuss your experiences with state-level music tests. Questions to consider in your discussion:

- Have you been required to take an NAEP test or some other form of state test for music?
- What are your feelings about standardized testing in the field of music?
- What other forms of tests you have experienced in music?
- Are these traditional or modern examples?

What has not been documented is whether teachers turned to existing music achievement tests during that time, tests such as Colwell's Music Achievement Tests (1969, 1970), the Iowa Tests of Music Literacy, or the Silver Burdett Music Competency Tests. Boyle and Radocy (1987) described these tests as follows: Colwell's four tests measure aural and visual skills such as pitch discrimination, interval discrimination, meter discrimination, major-minor mode discrimination, feeling for tonal center, auditory-visual discrimination, tonal memory, melody recognition, pitch recognition, instrument recognition, musical style, chord recognition, and cadence recognition. The Iowa Tests of Music Literacy written by Gordon (1970) are grouped into levels of difficulty. They have two sections: tonal concepts and rhythmic concepts, with aural perception, reading recognition, and notational understanding as part of each. The Silver Burdett test series was created by Colwell (1979) and, using a criterion-referenced method, measured perception of melody, rhythm, texture, form, tonality, and dynamics. These were tied directly to the objectives set forth in the Silver Burdett music series of books (Boyle & Radocy, 1987).

From 2010 onwards, various other states required that music teachers report data for student achievement growth. Wesolowski (2015) explained, step-by-step, how music teachers could collect, track, and report those data. Typically, this is required in US states using a student-learning objective framework with music teachers reporting the learning that occurs in their classrooms. Wesolowski clarified the process for teachers, specifying how to develop objectives, how to set meaningful learning targets, and how to identify the difference among global, educational, and instructional objectives. This was a landmark concept for music teachers at a time when very little guidance was given on how to assess students and collect data in their classrooms.

Classroom Assessments

Music teachers have been required over the past decade to provide student achievement data for their music classes. Part of this has been to satisfy their annual teaching evaluations, in which teachers are evaluated on their performance with several data sources: student-learning data, teaching observation data, and professional development reviews. Teachers continue to be asked to provide student achievement data from their classrooms. Classroom data allow teachers to have a clear sense of the strengths and weaknesses of their students at all times. Classroom assessments allow teachers to measure the growth and quality of their students' learning. Current classroom assessments in music education also have the potential to be culturally responsive (Boon, 2019) and reveal the holistic process of learning (Wiggins, 2015). In support of teaching for musical understanding, Wiggins advocates that "assessment of learning is embedded in and emerges from the learning experience" (p. 26).

Classroom assessments are typically used to provide data through observations, student products, and oral questioning (Russell & Airasian, 2012). Student observation allows teachers to garner data by observing how students perform their music, or work in groups, or even how students are asking questions. Observation can be informal but when they are planned and formal, such as a playing test, they can be used as information and data collection techniques. Student products can be artifacts such as homework, written assignments, worksheets, essays, music journals, composition projects, performance recordings, and portfolios, in addition to tests and quizzes. They can be developed as either selection items (select-response items where students choose an answer from choices supplied), constructed-response items (where students construct a response to a question), or performance tasks (where we ask student to complete a task). Data from all three forms of assessment give teachers information about students' skills and knowledge. Oral questioning is often used in classrooms, most often during instruction, as a formative informal assessment tool which can also illustrate metacognition, that is, how students are thinking about learning the music or skill that they are mastering. All three types of classroom assessments allow teachers to monitor student progress toward goals and allow for teachers to provide feedback.

In 2001 and 2003, the Music Educators National Conference (MENC) published two publications to assist teachers in assessing student skills in music classrooms. *Spotlight on Assessment in Music Education* (2001) grouped papers and ideas from educators in various music education associations around the USA, with the goal of sharing assessment expertise and ideas. Lindeman (2003) designed the *Benchmarks in Action* publication to assist music teachers in assessing the 1994 National Standards for Arts Education (MENC, 1994) in a standards-based approach. Benchmarks were presented for teachers to apply to their teaching setting and Brophy (2004) outlined a process that included "(1) organizing skills and knowledge to be assessed, (2) determining the appropriate assessment response mode, (3) selecting appropriate assessment materials, (4) developing an assessment task, and (5) developing scoring guides" (p. 1).

More recently, the Model Cornerstone Assessments (MCAs; see https://nafme.org/my-classroom/standards/mcas/) were published to accompany the 2014 National Core Arts Standards in Music. Burrack and Parkes (2018) coordinated the MCA development and pilot testing and led a team of researchers and music educators over the 2014–2015, 2015–2016, and 2016–2017 school years to develop the MCAs. The MCAs are described as providing:

> an instructional and assessment framework into which teachers integrate their curriculum to help measure student learning. The MCAs, designed by and for music educators, provide adaptable assessment tasks that assist students through the each of the artistic processes outlined in the 2014 Music Standards, allowing them to demonstrate the quality of learning associated with the performance standards. The assessment rubrics have been designed and tested to be used in the classroom by teachers. If administered as written by a practicing music educator, the MCAs are documented to be valid assessments of student learning and can reliably document student growth throughout a music program.
>
> (https://nafme.org/my-classroom/standards/mcas/)

The MCAs represent a shift in assessment for music education; a shift that moved from the traditional notion of assessing limited knowledge with a standardized test (for further reading, see Payne, Burrack, Parkes, & Wesolowski, 2019). This shift allows music teachers to select their curriculum and use formative and summative measures of student learning. The MCAs offer teachers a modern integrated approach to assessment, where assessments occur as part of instruction.

Many music teachers have not had an opportunity during their education or teacher preparation to learn about specific music assessment strategies. Researchers (e.g., LaCognata, 2013; McQuarrie & Sherwin, 2013; Russell & Austin, 2010) have indicated that teachers do not have equal experiences or exposure to quality music assessment instruction, with many teachers learning on-the-job. Parkes and Rawlings (2019) also found evidence that a sample of music teacher educators, those who teach future teachers, have varying levels of experience with music assessment in their own education. It may be possible that current students in music education have not experienced modern approaches to music assessment. Certainly, we have detailed descriptions of what band and orchestra directors and choral and elementary general educators do in their classrooms (see, respectively, Vaughan, 2019; Moss, Benham, & Pellegrino, 2019; Holcomb, 2019; Marlatt, 2019) so this is perhaps evidence that the field is moving to embrace assessment in music classrooms more fully.

Technology in Modern Assessment

There has been a noticeable response from the commercial technology sector with respect to using technology for educational assessment (see Massoth, 2019 for an overview). Consider the large standardized tests now available at computer testing centers, where tests are given on a computer. Rather than filling in circles on a Scantron page, test takers click, drag and drop, point, scroll, and hover their mouse to indicate correct answers. The administration of large-scale tests with computer-based testing may present more options for the ways in which questions are given to all test takers. Images can be presented in color, short sound and movie clips can be heard or viewed, and questions can be answered by clicking the correct answer or dragging a list into a correctly ranked order (for example, soft to loud: *piano, mezzopiano, mezzoforte, forte*). These technologies provide clear advantages, especially allowing tests to be more accommodating for learners with exceptionalities.

Computer-adaptive testing (CAT) is a modern development in computer-based testing, which essentially tailors questions to the test taker. The rise of CAT also relies on **item response theory (IRT)**. IRT allows item characteristics and test taker characteristics to be examined separately, allowing test creators to ascertain the differences between factors that impact the items (questions) and factors that impact the test taker. CAT allows the test-time difficulty to be targeted to the test taker ability. Stone and Davey (2011) suggest that the advantages of CAT are (a) it takes less time because it is tailored to the test taker; (b) there is less need for staffing; (c) there is more flexibility in in scheduling; (d) the collection of test taker data, such as how long it takes to answer a question or when or how often help was accessed; (e) more interaction with the test itself; (f) increased engagement with the test, as easier items are included sporadically to increase motivation and self-confidence; and (g) the implementation of accommodations such as color contrast, read-alouds, sign language inter-pretations, text highlighting, and content filters. Stone and Davey also outline the disadvantages, in which school districts are not able to afford computer-based testing technologies and there is also the assumption that all students are equally technologically literate. A serious issue to consider is that within CAT, test takers are not permitted to go back to items (ques-tions) already answered, as this might change the ability estimate. Despite these drawbacks, the use of CAT provides more efficiency than linear testing because fewer items are required to have evidence of measurement precision (Stone & Davey, 2011).

There has also been a rise in private, for-profit, web-based music tech-nology companies purporting to be able to assess and/or track student learning within an online setting. These web-based programs usually tie assessment to prescribed, provided on-demand online activities and cur-ricula. This is done via content delivery held in the cloud via the internet; however, the primary issue with these systems and products is the lack of educational psychometrics used to develop their items (questions). One of the main criticisms of these products is that there is little to no evidence of classical test theory analyses for their tests, and they do not use IRT; they do not publish reliability or validity estimates for their assessments in the way the Educational Testing Service (ETS) does. The assessments provided within these systems only target the objectives, when provided, from their on-demand content. These systems can be considered **Learning Management Systems,** systems that integrate software so teachers can cre-ate lessons and assignments and collect data to monitor student progress. Most offer sample lessons, curricula, automatic assessments, and other menus such as music scores, method book excerpts, and theory compo-nents for elementary, middle, and high school teachers. They often include music library access, gradebooks, and avenues to communicate with stu-dents (messaging or email) and provide methods via which students can submit work to teachers. Another criticism of these products is that they are an attempt to teacher-proof classrooms, claiming that any teacher can use the content to provide what might be seen as high-quality music education. These software systems should be carefully reviewed before being adopted or adapted into a music classroom; they should only be used when teach-ers select the materials most appropriate to the learners in front of them and when the materials selected adequately meet the musical outcomes teachers have set for their students within the appropriate developmental ranges. Bauer (2019) suggests that while technology can be used a tool for musical assessment, the basic principles of assessment must be adhered to when using backward design or universal design frameworks.

> *Learning Experience: If you don't already know the terms "backward design" or "universal design," conduct a keyword search using your library database. Use keywords such as "backward design," "backward planning," "backward mapping," "instruction outcomes," "universal design for learning," "universal design for instruction," and "universal instructional design." Use an additional author name search for "Wiggins and McTighe" and "David H. Rose and Ann Meyer."*
>
> *Once you have found materials explaining these two overarching terms, create a summary describing the similarities and differences between them.*

The landscape of educational assessment has historically been complex and yet is still developing. Brophy (2019) suggests that the field may be ready to embrace a set of international principles for assessment in music education. These principles include a shared language, quality norms, a clear purpose, ease of operability, alignment with curriculum, authenticity and appropriateness, social justice, and a valuing of assessment. In suggesting a set of literacy standards, Brophy raises the call to the profession to provide more information to music educators writ large about assessment and this book is, in part, a response to that call. Our understandings of learning, effective instructional practices, and assessment processes in music education are part of the current improvement paradigm. Accountability policy is, to some extent, still driving the current changes occurring in music classrooms today. We need to view assessment processes as simply part of excellent teaching and learning; assessment processes (such as measurement and evaluation) used with modern approaches allow learners to improve and allow teachers to adjust their instruction, for both short- and long-term instructional goals.

References

Bauer, W. I. (2019). Assessing music learning with technology. In T. Brophy (Ed.), *The Oxford handbook of assessment policy and practice in music education* (Vol. 2, pp. 878–899). New York, NY: Oxford University Press.

Boon, E. T. (2019). Culturally responsive assessment in music education. In T. Brophy (Ed.), *The Oxford handbook of assessment policy and practice in music education* (Vol. 2, pp. 737–753). New York, NY: Oxford University Press.

Boyle, J. D., & Radocy, R. E. (1987). *Measurement and evaluation of musical experiences.* New York, NY: Schirmer Books, Macmillan Inc.

Brophy, T. S. (2004). Developing and implementing standards-based assessments. In C. Lindemann (Ed.), *Benchmarks in action: A guide to standards-based assessment in music* (pp. 11–16). Reston, VA: MENC and the National Association for Music Education.

Brophy, T. S. (2019). Assessment in music education: The state of the art. In T. Brophy (Ed.), *The Oxford handbook of assessment policy and practice in music education* (Vol. 2, pp. 904–931). New York, NY: Oxford University Press.

Burrack, F., & Parkes, K. A. (Eds.). (2018). *Applying Model Cornerstone Assessments in K – 12 music: A research-supported approach*. Lanham, MD: Rowman & Littlefield.

Colwell, R. (1969). *Music achievement tests 1 and 2*. Chicago: Follett Educational Corporation.

Colwell, R. (1970). *Music achievement tests 3 and 4*. Chicago: Follett Educational Corporation.

Colwell, R. (1979). *Silver Burdett music competency tests*. Morristown, NJ: Silver Burdett.

Giordano, G. (2005). *How testing came to dominate American schools: The history of educational assessment*. New York, NY: Peter Lang Publishing Inc.

Gordon, E. E. (1970). *Iowa tests of music literacy*. Iowa City: Bureau of Educational Research and Service, University of Iowa.

Henry, M. L. (2019). The Texas music assessment: Grassroots development of a statewide music test. In T. Brophy (Ed.), *The Oxford handbook of assessment policy and practice in music education* (Vol. 2, pp. 209–232). New York, NY: Oxford University Press.

Holcomb, A. D. (2019). Assessment practices of American choral music educators. In T. Brophy (Ed.), *The Oxford handbook of assessment policy and practice in music education* (Vol. 2, pp. 379–400). New York, NY: Oxford University Press.

Hudson, M., & Gates, K. (2019). Assessment in music education: A Colorado partnership. In T. Brophy (Ed.), *The Oxford handbook of assessment policy and practice in music education* (Vol. 2, pp. 233–254). New York, NY: Oxford University Press.

Joseph, A. R. (2019). Washington state's classroom-based performance assessments: Formative and summative design for music education. In T. Brophy (Ed.), *The Oxford handbook of assessment policy and practice in music education* (Vol. 2, pp. 177–208). New York, NY: Oxford University Press.

Kelly, S. N., Cummings, B., & Gordon, M. G. (2019). The Florida Performing Fine Arts Assessment Project. In T. Brophy (Ed.), *The Oxford handbook of assessment policy and practice in music education* (pp. 123–142). New York, NY: Oxford University Press.

LaCognata, J. (2013). Current student assessment practices of high school band directors in the United States. In T. Brophy (Ed.), *Music assessment across cultures and continents* (pp. 109–128). Chicago, IL: GIA Publications.

Lewis, A. A., Burgess, Y., & Fan, X. (2019). The South Carolina arts assessment program. In T. Brophy (Ed.), *The Oxford handbook of assessment policy and practice in music education* (Vol. 2, pp. 281–306). New York, NY: Oxford University Press.

Lindeman, C. (2003). *Benchmarks in action: A guide to standards-based assessment in music education.* Reston, VA: MENC and the National Association for Music Education.

Marlatt, J. (2019). Assessment practices of American elementary general music classrooms. In T. Brophy (Ed.), *The Oxford handbook of assessment policy and practice in music education* (Vol. 2, pp. 423–444). New York, NY: Oxford University Press.

Massoth, D. (2019). Technical issues related to computerized music assessment performance. In T. Brophy (Ed.), *The Oxford handbook of assessment policy and practice in music education* (Vol. 2, pp. 855–875). New York, NY: Oxford University Press.

McQuarrie, S., & Sherwin, R. (2013). Assessment in music education: Relationships between training, experience, and common practice. In T. Brophy (Ed.), *Music assessment across cultures and continents* (pp. 141–152). Chicago, IL: GIA Publications.

MENC. (1994). *National Standards for Arts Education: What every young American should know and be able to do in the arts.* Reston, VA: MENC and the National Association for Music Education.

MENC. (2001). *Spotlight on assessment in music education.* Reston, VA: MENC and the National Association for Music Education.

Moss, K., Benham, S., & Pellegrino, K. (2019). Assessment practices of American orchestra directors. In T. Brophy (Ed.), *The Oxford handbook of assessment policy and practice in music education* (Vol. 2, pp. 401–422). New York, NY: Oxford University Press.

National Assessment of Educational Progress. (2016). *Nation's report card-arts assessment.* Retrieved from www.nationsreportcard.gov/arts_2016/

Orzolek, D. C. (2019, March). *A framework for evaluation music teacher evaluation systems. Research paper presented at the Advancing Music Education Through Assessment: 7th International Symposium on Assessment in Music Education.* Gainesville, Florida.

Parkes, K. A., & Rawlings, J. R. (2019). The preparation of music teacher educators to use and teach assessment. *Contributions to Music Education, 45,* 145–165.

Payne, D. A. (2003). *Applied educational assessment.* Belmont, CA: Wadsworth Publishing.

Payne, P. D., Burrack, F., Parkes, K. A., & Wesolowski, B. (2019). An emerging process of assessment in music education. *Music Educators Journal, 105*(3), 36–44. https://doi.org/10.1177/0027432118818880

Pizmony-Levy, O. (2018). The OptOut movement is gaining ground, quietly. *The Hechinger Report.* Retrieved October 20, 2018 from https://hechingerreport.org/opinion-the-opt-out-movement-is-gaining-ground-quietly/

Russell, J. A., & Austin, J. R. (2010). Assessment practices of secondary music teachers. *Journal of Research in Music Education, 58,* 37–54. doi:10.1177/0022429409360062

Russell, M. K., & Airasian, P. W. (2012). *Classroom assessment: Concepts and applications.* New York, NY: McGraw-Hill.

Shaw, R. D., & Taggart, C. C. (2019). Measuring student learning in Michigan: The Michigan arts education instruction and assessment project. In

T. S. Brophy (Ed.), *The Oxford handbook of assessment policy and practice in music education* (Vol. 2, pp. 255–279). New York, NY: Oxford University Press.

Sherwin, R. G., & McQuarrie, S. H. (2019). The impact of state testing on American music classrooms. In T. Brophy (Ed.), *The Oxford handbook of assessment policy and practice in music education* (Vol. 2, pp. 21–36). New York, NY: Oxford University Press.

Stone, E., & Davey, T. (2011). Computer-adaptive testing for students with disabilities: A review of the literature. *ETS Research Report RR-11–32*. Princeton, NJ: ETS. Retrieved from https://onlinelibrary.wiley.com/doi/epdf/10.1002/j.2333-8504.2011.tb02268.x

Stufflebeam, D. L. (2000). The CIPP model for evaluation. In D. L. Stufflebeam, G. F. Madaus, & T. Kellaghan (Eds.), *Evaluation models: Viewpoints on educational and human service evaluation* (2nd ed., pp. 279–317). Boston: Kluwer Academic.

Swanson, R. K., & Shepherd, P. E. (2019). Kentucky policies and practices for assessment in music education: Past, present and future. In T. Brophy (Ed.), *The Oxford handbook of assessment policy and practice in music education* (Vol. 2, pp. 143–176). New York, NY: Oxford University Press.

US Department of Education. (2009). *The race to the top begins*. Retrieved from www.ed.gov/news/speeches/race-top-begins

Vaughan, C. J. (2019). Assessment practices of American band directors. In T. Brophy (Ed.), *The Oxford handbook of assessment policy and practice in music education* (Vol. 2, pp. 351–378). New York, NY: Oxford University Press.

Wesolowski, B. (2015). Tracking student achievement in music performance: Developing student learning objectives for growth model assessments. *Music Educators Journal*, 102(1), 39–47. Retrieved from www.jstor.org/stable/24755629

Wiggins, J. (2015). *Teaching for musical understanding*. New York, NY: Oxford University Press.

2 The Purpose of Assessment

Frederick Burrack and Kelly A. Parkes

Chapter Overview

This chapter focuses on the purpose and importance of assessment in schools. Addressed will be overarching principles of assessment as a process integrated in educational practice, general understanding and terminology associated with defining expectations of student learning, assessment as measures that differentiate qualities of learning, considerations of assessment as formative, and how this relates to summative evaluations that lead to practices such as grading.

Learning Expectations for the Chapter

- Define the meaning of learning outcomes and the expectations of student achievement that guide curricular and instructional decisions.
- Identify the differences between grading and assessment.
- Understand common assessment terminology and their uses.
- Recognize principles of assessment as they apply to schools.

Essential Questions for the Chapter

- What is meant by learning outcomes and why is it important that they are defined?
- Why isn't traditional grading sufficient as a process of assessment?
- What terminology is important to know?

Introduction

The purpose of an assessment process is to make the expectations of student learning explicit and evident. The process includes systematically gathering, analyzing, and interpreting evidence to determine how well demonstrations of student learning match the level of learning quality expected and to use the resulting information to document, explain, and improve performance (Angelo, 1995). As explained in Chapter 1, the historical landscape for assessment has been complex and is still developing. Understandings of learning, effective instructional practices, assessment processes in an improvement paradigm, and responsive policy is driving the current changes occurring in education. The need for assessment processes in classrooms is clearly explained by Fautley (2010): "Assessment assists students to improve, illustrates what they have learned, provides evidence for the teacher to guide instruction, and provides information for both school and parent" (p. 60). In considering assessment as it relates to music teaching and learning in our classrooms, when we measure learning, we become better teachers (Popham, 2003). These considerations of assessment in schools align with Conway (2015) who suggests that assessment interacts with teaching, curriculum, and learning.

Unfortunately, assessment in schools has been narrowly used to judge achievement of students, or the quality of a teacher, or the excellence of a school system. Most often assessment for K-12 music programs or individual courses has been administered as performance of ensembles and often compared to current norms through regional or state music festivals. Other forms of program assessment markers, such as the method books used or difficulty of performance literature, are used erroneously to define the quality of an entire K-12 music program. In music classrooms, teachers sometimes monitor student involvement during classroom activities or whole-class performance as a determination of learning. In the process of teaching, observing signs of understanding or confusion in students enables teachers to adjust course activities and improve student learning. While these processes effectively provide impressions of learning, direct evidence of individual students' learning reflective of defined learning expectations is missing.

Following the development of the 1994 National Standards for Music, assessment began to be considered with increasing importance in K-12 music programs. In 2014, the National Standards for Music were revised by the National Coalition for Core Arts Standards (NCCAS). MCAs were designed, and pilot tested, to provide a framework allowing K-12 school music programs to integrate relevant and current curriculum. Assessments can interact with decisions and observations that the teacher makes during the course of the music lesson (Fautley, 2009). Indicators of learning during instruction that obviously impact music teaching have not been considered means of assessment. As seen in the MCAs, classroom assessments become key components to the processes of performing, creating, and responding and are opportunities for teachers to make a range of decisions that help students progress in music learning. Student work in music classes and lessons can and should effectively be used as assessments by teachers (see Figure 2.1).

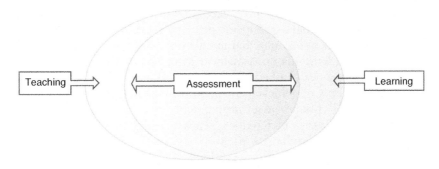

Figure 2.1 Interaction of assessment with teaching and learning

There are some aspects of what we teach that are purely developmental and will not be a part of assessment, and there are some things that students learn that are beyond the capacity to assess in school, but the majority of what students learn can be assessed through the actions students undertake in a music class. These actions demonstrate the ways students understand and apply what has been taught. These are the opportunities music teachers can use to assess learning.

Recent Developments in Learning Outcomes

Assessment has three key activities: (a) articulating learning goals and Course Learning Objectives (CLOs) to guide curricular and instructional decisions; (b) assessing students' learning in a systematic and direct way; and (c) applying information uncovered by the assessments to improve student learning success. It is a common objective in many K-12 music programs to develop student skills with a goal to produce high-quality ensemble performance. Beyond performance, tasks through which music students demonstrate learning might include (a) individual or groups of students composing a piece using classroom instruments; (b) a student helping other students in a sectional on ways to phrase a melodic line; (c) a section leader pointing out where to breathe in a song being rehearsed; (d) a student creating and appropriately leading an ensemble warm-up; (e) students researching and writing program notes for an upcoming concert; or (f) the response from students when discussing what atmosphere is created by a musical piece they are performing. All of these, and many more, are assessments of learned material and applied skills (Fautley, 2009). Consideration of specific measurable criteria are found in many scoring devices. Performance skills are commonly defined in scoring devices for contest and festival, but not often applied in a formal assessment process in K-12 school music programs. Expectations of student

learning are often defined by applied skills observed in student performance, but there are many more ways that students can demonstrate
music learning. Formal assessments of many types can be designed as
a means to document learning that has already occurred, ex post facto.

Current considerations of assessment recognize that nearly all classroom music activities can be used as a form of assessment, whether as
formal evaluations of achievement or to provide information to guide
future learning. A common assessment practice in music is observations of
students during classroom activities. Teachers use these observations to
make decisions as to what to teach or reteach. Recent considerations
of assessment accept scored observations as a primary focus of assessment, both as a judgement of achievement and to gain information for
teaching. In any assessment practice, proactive considerations of defining
the expected learning in advance of instructional content selection and
teaching is now a common function of assessment (Wiggins & McTighe,
2005). Instead of creating assessments to evaluate whether students recall
what has been taught, backward design (Wiggins & McTighe, 2005) first
defines what is to be learned before teaching commences. Assessment of
learning outcomes focuses on how students make sense of what has been
taught and how they integrate their personal understandings into musical artistic processes. Designated learning outcomes are used as the basis
for planning the instructional content and teaching processes. In music
classes and ensembles, learning outcomes are the foundation for selecting
the musical repertoire through which students develop the expected outcomes. Then instruction is sequentially designed to enable musical experiences that lead to these learning outcomes. The example in Figure 2.2
provides a visual sequence for a music ensemble course.

Defining learning outcomes and developmentally sequencing learning across an entire K-12 music program are foundational in a program
assessment plan. As will be more fully described in Chapter 3, broad
student learning goals that encompass all levels of learning reflect the
mission of the program and provide a framework for the measurable

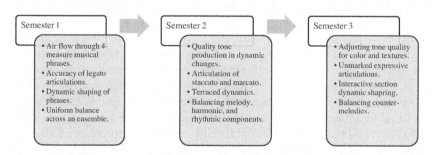

Figure 2.2 Sample instructional planning sequence for the skill of performing in
an ensemble

learning outcomes that identify students' progress toward the learning goals. Instructional tasks integrated in coursework are the means through which students demonstrate the quality of their learning (knowledge, skills, and dispositions) and become part of the flow of a classroom lesson. Designing an effective assessment plan requires the music teacher to consider the goals of student learning and to define how these program goals are applied appropriately at developmental levels. Course-embedded assessments are musical tasks and experiences within classroom activities that allow students to demonstrate the quality of their learning. In the assessment plan, teachers use collected scores from student learning assessments to differentiate qualities of achievement in order to guide future planning of teaching sequences, progressively guide students toward the achievement expectations, and provide a picture of student learning across a music program.

One of the most important decisions that can result from defining learning outcomes across a K-12 school music program is the alignment of learning objectives that occur within specific courses with appropriate course content (music selections or repertoire). Content of classroom and ensemble courses should be selected to intentionally expand knowledge, understanding, and skills of intended learning outcomes. It is also important to identify how and to what extent students are expected to demonstrate musical learning so these outcomes can be attained through the musical content selected. Thoughtful consideration of students' developmental learning is foundational to enhancing musical constructs and skills in students across their experiences in a music program. When learning outcomes and consideration of assessments precede music selection and instructional planning, the music teacher is able to intentionally design teaching plans tied to the progressive development of student learning within a music course. The 2014 National Standards for Music provide a developmental consideration of learning through experiences in a K-12 school music program.

Evaluation and Assessment

When discussing assessment of learning, you may have this question in mind: *How will the assessment help me grade my students?* Schools have an expectation that teachers document and report student learning. Assessment, as a process, is often confused with grading. In fact, the terms are often used synonymously, which in many ways is incorrect. Assessment in music is the process through which teachers interpret student learning as exemplified in the artistic processes of performing, creating, and responding so teachers and the students themselves can pursue consistently higher levels of achievement. Grading, on the other hand, is the assigning of a mark (or grade) to indicate overall fulfillment of expectations at one point in time. The process of assessment utilizes tasks through which students demonstrate what has been learned. Teachers use some form of the scoring devices to collect data on student learning to compare, analyze, and making instructional decisions. For example, an assessment task and scoring device can be seen when a student plays their instrument for a teacher who scores the event with a rubric. A measurement tool for music learning is most effective when it simultaneously assesses multiple skills and knowledge components in order to fully represent music learning. Resulting data, in turn, can be used by teachers to enhance their approach to instruction, motivate student progress, and improve musical achievement. In assessment, specific expectations guide implementation of strategies to collect and score observable achievements.

Unfortunately, with grading, busy music educators preparing their students for performance often develop grading strategies that do not reflect the full spectrum of learning and are implemented as a segmented component from the tasks at hand. Grades instead should be determined by collecting and combining multiple scores into a mark or set of marks that represent the full extent of music learning. Summative grading is the process of rating student performance of knowledge or skills and coding the results as numbers, letters, or percentages. It is difficult for the grading process to reflect learning in music because a single letter grade on an assignment cannot differentiate achievement of the multiple qualities of learning that are exhibited. Furthermore, a course grade generalizes a great deal of information about student learning into one single letter or number. A single grade does not provide sufficient information for a student or teacher to identify specific qualities of learning to guide decisions toward learning or programmatic improvements (see Figure 2.3).

If our responsibility as music educators is to help students become self-sufficient musicians, then an educative perspective of assessment focuses on ways to improve student learning (Payne, 2003). In an assessment process, nearly all musical experiences consist of multiple learning outcomes simultaneously demonstrated. Assessment scoring devices that can disaggregate

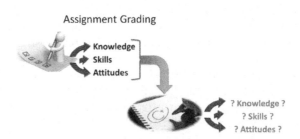

Figure 2.3 Example of the inadequacy of a single grade for identifying specific achievement

Outcome Assessment

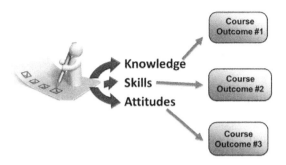

Figure 2.4 Example of disaggregating assessment results by outcome

achievement by scoring individual criteria demonstrated in the assessment measure are the most effective. Instead of averaging proficiencies into a single score, an assessment process should identify qualities of learning for each learning criterion (see Figure 2.4).

Learning Experience: Pair up with a classmate and use the following worksheet to discuss experiences where you have been part of an assessment process that provides information of progress toward expected learning as compared to a scoring evaluation for grading. What are the differences and similarities? Then describe how assessments can be useful in assigning a grade and whether grading alone can provide the same educational value.

Assessment

- _____
- _____
- _____

Evaluations for Grading

- _____
- _____
- _____

When scored and reported in this manner, information can be used to identify specific learning deficiencies to guide improved learning. The value of assessment is the specificity of achievement per learning outcome and its component criteria to expose specific learning achieved and uncover unattained learning needs that can guide curricular and instructional decisions within courses and across a K-12 school music program.

Assessment Principles

Stiggins (2002) suggested that the absence of assessment constitutes a crisis for learning. Assessment, as a process, is part of effective instruction and an essential part of the teaching and learning cycle. One of the primary principles of assessment is that instruction and assessment must be interactive. What is assessed must reflect what has been taught and what is learned from assessment must inform what will be taught. In this assessment paradigm, assessment and instruction should hold a common purpose, which is to teach and to inform.

This conception of assessment leads to another principle that comprehends the importance of context in design, analysis, and use. There is no one-size-fits-all assessment in process or measure. What one teacher uses to assess learning in students is not necessarily appropriate for another teacher to use unless the context of course objectives, assessed criteria, contextual purpose, and students' developmental level are the same. This principle addresses three features of assessment: (a) use multiple techniques in both structured and unstructured settings, (b) acceptance that students demonstrate learning in unique ways, and (c) recognition of how context (student and learning environment) interacts with the quality of student achievement. When educators engage in the process of assessment, using a variety of measures will allow students to demonstrate learning in the ways that make sense to them. The ultimate purpose of assessment is to uncover how students make sense of and apply what has been taught, in contrast to testing whether students recall what has been presented to them. Assessment instruments (assessments such as tests, rubrics, checklists, performances, and portfolios) need to be designed to uncover the multiple ways that learning can be represented. The purpose of assessment is to guide instruction, expose misunderstandings, uncover factors that influence learning, and to inform the extent to which an end goal or outcome has been achieved.

In music classrooms, many teachers are asked to create their own assessments to illustrate student learning. The beliefs that support a culture of assessment in K-12 school music programs are particularly helpful leading toward the benefits that can result in effective and efficient assessment processes. It is important to recognize that assessments are ongoing and integrated with instruction, in contrast to an after-instruction evaluation; that learning expectations are to guide instruction as well as for students to actively evaluate their own progress and achievement; and that assessments of student learning are useful to assist teachers in evaluating their teaching (Sheppard, 2000). Giving students more responsibility for their own learning enhances ownership and motivation to learn. The foundation for student motivation is their internalization or ownership of the expected outcome. Learning outcomes and feedback from multiple forms of assessment inform students of where they are relative to the mastery of the various aspects of music learning so they can effectively focus their efforts. Assessment must be educative to both the learner and the teacher (Wiggins, 1998).

Music classrooms are especially fortunate to facilitate engagement in performance assessments. A performance-based assessment is an assessment built on applying what is known through doing. Terminology such as *direct assessment* and *authentic assessment* are used to strengthen the notion that performance-based assessment tasks are indicative of real life. The term performance-based can be confusing in music because the word performance refers not only to how students apply learning but also to the act of performing a piece of music. For example, a composition can be considered a performance-based assessment because this assessment task provides evidence of the student's ability to compose but also demonstrates "knowing" chords, notation, musical forms, and many other aspects of learning. Performance-based assessments allow for engagement with the processes of music, generate a product or performance, and provide evidence contextualized in a realistic setting. Authentic assessments are part of good teaching and learning interactions in a K-12 school music program (see Figure 2.5).

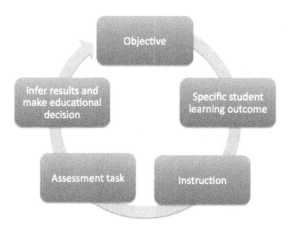

Figure 2.5 Assessment position in one instructional cycle

The steps for how to apply this instructional cycle of assessment will be described later in this text. It is important at this point to recognize how this structure of instructional planning can be useful to inform the teacher in planning content and instructional strategies and to consider ways that students can better understand their progress toward learning outcomes.

Learning Experience: Divide into groups that focus on specific areas and levels in a music program (e.g., early elementary, middle school instrumental, high school choral). Each group should generate a series of learning expectations and explore how students might demonstrate what and how they have learned.

- Step 1: Identify several general learning expectations that should result from students' involvement across a music program.
- Step 2: Specify a music class in the program and define how the learning expectations might be defined in this class.
- Step 3: Discuss specific examples of how students might demonstrate that they have learned.

Summary

Student learning assessment fulfills a purpose of exposing qualities of learning, proficiency, or achievement particular to specific learning expectations of a music class or entire K-12 music program. With increasing specificity of disaggregation into the criteria assessed, the process becomes increasingly useful to guide instructional decisions that can impact student learning for both individuals as well as groups of students in a music program. Assessment measures that are scaled by difficulty and/or complexity across a curriculum can contribute important information about developmental achievement that can lead to instructional and curricular improvements. Assessment processes embedded into instruction and with authentic application of the outcome often result in the most useful information to guide instruction, motivate students, and determine program effectiveness. This is the conceptual understanding of assessment that guides music programs as we progress further into the 21st century.

Preparatory Experience for Future Chapters

Assessment Terminology

Web search for the key phrases "educational assessment" and "music assessment." Scan several of the links and make note of terms that you recognize and those that you don't. In a class discussion, share both lists and discuss the meaning of these terms.

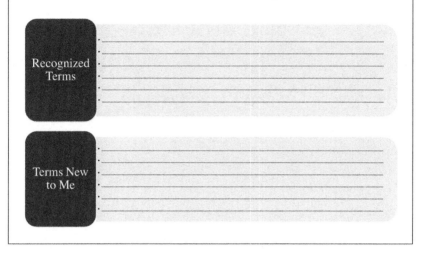

References and Additional Reading

Angelo, T. A. (1995). Reassessing and defining assessment. *American Association for Higher Education Bulletin, 48,* 7–9.

Conway, C. M. (2015). *Musicianship-focused curriculum and assessment.* Chicago, IL: GIA Publications.

Fautley, M. (2009). Assessment for learning in music. In J. Evans & C. Philpott (Eds.), *A practical guide to teaching music in the secondary school.* London, England: Taylor and Francis Group.

Fautley, M. (2010). *Assessment in music education.* New York: Oxford University Press.

Payne, D. A. (2003). *Educational assessment.* Belmont, CA: Wadsworth Publishing.

Popham, W. J. (2003). *Test better, teach better: The instructional role of assessment.* Alexandria, VA: Association for Supervision and Curriculum Development.

Sheppard, L. (2000). The role of assessment in learning culture. *Educational Researcher, 29*(7), 4–14.

Stiggins, R. J. (2002). Assessment crisis: The absence of assessment for learning. *Phi Delta Kappan, 83*, 758–765.

Wiggins, G. (1998). *Educative assessment: Designing assessments to inform and improve student performance.* San Francisco, CA: Jossey-Bass.

Wiggins, G., & McTighe, J. (2005). *Understanding by design.* Alexandria, VA: Association for Supervision and Curriculum Development.

3 Assessment Across a K-12 School Music Program

Frederick Burrack and Kelly A. Parkes

Chapter Overview

Chapter 2 provided a rationale as to why formal assessment of intentional learning outcomes is important for teaching and learning; however, it is also important for entire school music programs. This chapter continues with a framework for how to integrate a student learning assessment process into a K-12 music program. This begins with developing overarching goals, defining programmatic and course-specific learning objectives, and suggesting how to write clear and effective learning objectives. The chapter concludes with guidance in aligning goals and outcomes, integrating the assessment plan across a K-12 music program curriculum, and suggestions on establishing a culture of assessment within the context of a school.

Learning Expectations for the Chapter

- Develop skills in defining developmentally sequenced course learning objectives (CLOs), overarching learning outcomes, and programmatic learning goals.
- Develop an assessment structure that aligns with the context of a K-12 school music program.
- Plan a sustainable assessment process for a K-12 school music program.

Essential Questions for the Chapter

- How do learning goals, program outcomes, and course-based learning objectives fit into an assessment structure?
- How can outcomes be sequentially aligned across a K-12 school music program?

Why Should Teachers Assess Student Learning Across a K-12 Music Program?

Most agree that what music students learn in schooling is central to subsequent engagement and satisfaction in music, satisfaction in life, the nation's cultural development, and building healthy and civically engaged members of communities. As mentioned in Chapter 2, Fautley (2010) and Popham (2003) gave us several reasons why we should assess the learning that occurs in K-12 school music programs within individual classes and courses and across the entire program. Assessment is part of a good and effective K-12 music program because it helps both learner and teacher know the extent to which things has been learned and what yet needs to be developed. The process of assessment informs teaching and exposes the extent to which learning has occurred. Without assessment, unanswered questions remain as to what and how well students have learned. Effective assessments are also useful to provide feedback to students about what they are doing well and in what areas they should strive to improve. For schooling, assessment provides summative evaluations at particular moments in students' learning development. Documented information about student learning can also assist teachers in improving their own teaching (Bernard & Abramo, 2019)

Some music educators resist defining and systematically assessing student learning in music because they feel it can reduce a complex and creative process to a list of simplified and unconnected tasks. It is important to remember that effective teaching, learning, and assessment are not about attaining facts or independent skills; they are about engaging students in ways to foster a genuine love of music; an internal drive to analyze, interpret, and improve; and to attain higher-order proficiencies. Teachers should also be curious to understand how their teaching impacts student learning. The evidence of learning from assessments should be foundational information for teaching. The challenge is to gather evidence of proficiencies in ways that preserve the complexity of making and experiencing music. Identifying what students learn helps direct instructional decisions and leads to alignment of pedagogy and curricular content across the music program within a school. Documenting learning and using that evidence to improve student learning and program performance is a process that can improve student success.

Assessment Structure

Music educators work to create affective learning environments through instructional musical experiences that can lead to involvement with music beyond the classroom. For this reason, a structured assessment process should be an important part of music teaching and of long-term music program planning. A formal assessment framework built across a school music program curriculum helps teachers focus on student learning.

A K-12 school music program's assessment framework begins with overarching Program Learning Goals (PLG) that encompass learning at all levels and courses. These goals are selected based upon the program's mission and educational focus. They are to be addressed appropriately at each grade level and within courses across the entire music program. Examples of school music program learning goals may be:

1. Develop musical literacy and technical proficiency to the point where students concentrate on the musical message being expressed rather than on the means of expression.
2. Make music alone and with others, improving their self-concept and contribution to a larger group of human beings and perceiving their value within the school and community.
3. Be acquainted with diverse musical styles enabling them to transmit the value of our cultural heritage to succeeding generations and to understand the world's musical heritage.

Program goals can be addressed at all grade levels and in all courses in a music program, be it second-grade general music, middle school choir, or high school theory class.

Program goals are broad and not sufficiently specific to be measured. Each of a school music program's learning goals often consist of one or more Program Learning Outcomes (PLOs) that clearly define the assessable components of the goal to be appropriately taught and assessed across the music program. They are the road map for the curriculum and are the foundation on which assessment is built (Martell, 2005). Examples of PLOs for the first goal stated above could be as follows:

- Students can accurately sight-read printed music of difficulty and complexity appropriate for the developmental level of the course enrolled.
- Students demonstrate proficiency of technical aspects relevant to the musical medium involved in the music class and the level of expectation defined by the course level.
- Students can determine and musically apply expressive intent of the composer, musical style/genre, or creative goals of the musical event.

Each PLO is addressed at an appropriate developmental level specifically interpreted within Course Learning Objectives (CLO). CLOs identify specific, observable behaviors, actions, and cognitions related to a PLO that music teachers will use to describe, monitor, and assess student achievement. CLOs clearly define how students demonstrate course level expectations as indicators of learning for the PLO (Figure 3.1).

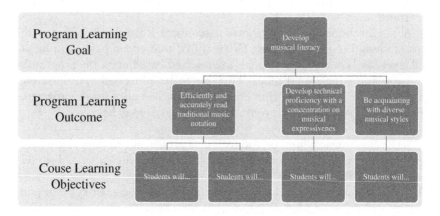

Figure 3.1 Segment of an assessment framework for a music program

CLOs

- Are derived from PLOs and indicators of program learning goals.
- Describe what students will demonstrate as evidence of meeting a PLO.
- Are observable and can be measured.
- Are realistic, attainable, and challenging.
- Contain action verbs specifying the complexity of the expectation.
- Are written in simple language for the student to understand.
- Describe what students do in contrast to what teachers do.

Music teachers use PLOs to guide development of CLOs. The expectations for student learning defined in courses by CLOs help focus decisions on music literature selection and guide decisions for designing instructional activities and learning assessments. When PLOs and CLOs guide curriculum, the overall goals for learning easily align across the program.

In addition to guiding what students are asked to do in class, the aligned assessment measures document the progress students make toward mastery of the PLOs as they move through the program. Instructionally embedded assessment tasks are a means of identifying achievement across a continuum of learning. Course-embedded tasks designed for students to demonstrate the quality of learning for CLOs often come directly from classroom activities with which a scoring device measures levels of achievement. Assessment tasks can also be derived from external sources such as the MCAs for the National Standards for Music (see https://nafme. org/my-classroom/standards/mcas/). The MCAs are assessment frameworks created to identify the quality of learning for each Performance Standard of the Process Components that define performing, creating, and responding. The design of these assessment frameworks integrates the school curricular content into the assessment and score achievement with rubrics that have been shown to have acceptable evidence of validity and reliability. The primary purpose of CLOs is to identify the achievement level toward learning outcomes through applying a measuring tool (such as a rubric) to score students demonstrating the expected music learning in the way that they and their school curriculum find relevant, whether it be performing, creating, or responding. Program assessment is an ongoing process that collects and monitors CLO results for each PLO to identify the contribution of the curriculum and instruction on student development of the learning defined as essential.

Since music learning can take many forms, assessment tasks must be sufficiently flexible to allow students to explore and demonstrate their learning in ways that make sense to them and within their capability while clearly demonstrating the expected learning. In designing tasks and their scoring devices, it is important for a teacher to identify what it means for a student to be successful, with sufficient differentiation to also expose deficiencies in student learning. Exposing learning deficiencies can inform teachers when to go back and reteach or to progress toward new or enhanced outcomes. Documenting student progress over time, for each outcome, provides a picture of learning for individual students, as well as for the cohort of students progressing through the school music program. The goal is to provide a wide range of evidence for teachers to use in making curricular and instructional decisions that can impact student learning and musical success.

An effective assessment process can provide information to improve communication among music teachers about what their students are doing and learning. In the sharing of learning outcomes and assessable criteria, students will have a better understanding of expectations that can be used to guide and motivate their developmental practices. Although such discussions should be a regular component within school music programs, without assessments that differentiate qualities of student learning, these discussions often lack supportive data to give meaning. A series of practical music tasks used as student learning assessments provides the broadest range of evidence upon which teachers and students can make judgements as to the best course of action for instruction and practice (Fautley, 2010). Student learning viewed longitudinally across a school music program has the capacity to affect decisions that teachers make for long-term goals.

Developing Goals and PLOs

"The key to assessment lies in determining the objectives of instruction and designing curricula to achieve them. Every teacher should know exactly what it is that he or she wants the students to know and be able to do" (Lehman, 1992, p. 57). The first step in a program assessment plan is to define the overall learning goals for the program. These goals will be used to guide the development of PLOs and the curriculum across

Program Goals   **Program Learning Outcomes**

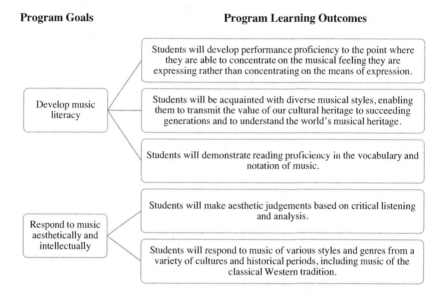

Figure 3.2 Example of goals and component PLOs

grade levels and course, which are the CLOs. Program goals are overarching expectations such as "develop music literacy" or "respond to music
aesthetically and intellectually." These broad statements are used to guide
the development of more specific PLOs that can be used by teachers across
the music program to unify the curriculum. Defined PLOs give teachers
an overview of student learning across a program and insight into how
their classroom activities are contributing to each area of student learning.
Each learning goal might include more than one specific learning outcome
in order to address specific components. For example, see Figure 3.2.

The 2014 National Standards for Music offer broad learning statements called "Enduring Understandings" (https://nafme.org/wp-content/
files/2014/06/Core-Music-Standards-EUs-EQs-Definitions.pdf). These
statements summarize important learnings that are central musical experience and have lasting value beyond the classroom. They are useful to
guide the development of program learning goals. The Process Components provided in the 2014 National Standards provide guidance toward
defining PLOs because they have been developed for application across a
curriculum. The key is to define PLOs that can be taught and measured
at various levels of development across the curriculum. For examples of
outcomes that are so general that they are difficult to measure as well as
focused outcomes that can more effectively be developed and assessed,
see Figure 3.3.

The primary purpose of clearly defined PLOs is to guide alignment
and clarity of the developmental CLOs integrated in courses across a

INEFFECTIVE EXAMPLES OF MEASURABLE OUTCOMES	**Knowledge**: The student will understand the relationship between theory and music performance.
	Skill: Perform accurately.
	Attitude: The student will enjoy music.

EFFECTIVE EXAMPLES OF MEASURABLE OUTCOMES	**Knowledge**: Students will demonstrate a working knowledge of appropriate historical and stylistic performance practices through analysis and supported performance.
	Skill: Students will demonstrate technical skills requisite for artistic self-expression in at least one primary performance area with an ability to perform from a cross-section of that repertoire, to read at sight with fluency, and to perform in a variety of solo and ensemble settings.
	Attitude: Students will work independently and cooperatively on a variety of musical problems by combining their capabilities in performance; aural, verbal, and visual analysis; composition and improvisation; and history and repertoire.

Figure 3.3 Examples of PLOs

program's curriculum. Alignment and intentionally sequenced CLOs will enable a cohesive curriculum to enhance student knowledge, skills, dispositions, and overall learning. Before teachers define their CLOs, it is important for all teachers in the program to consider how difficulty and complexity within each PLO are developed across the courses in the program. Creating a matrix of learning enables teachers to recognize intended learning development sequence across courses. This structure guides instructional planning, decisions of course content, and development of tasks through which students demonstrate qualities of learning and defines benchmark expectations used for grading.

Defining CLOs

CLOs are explicit statements of what student are expected to learn in courses reflecting the expectations within PLOs. These objectives provide a focused view of the broader PLOs appropriate for students' developmental level and the course context. Once defined, the CLOs help music teachers select appropriate literature and course content that will lead toward the intended learning, focus learning experiences designed help students achieve the CLO expectations, and define the assessments integrated in coursework. When provided to students, CLOs help motivate toward learning expectations.

When defining learning objectives, it is important to consider the depth of learning expected appropriate for the assessment task. The CLOs should clearly define how deeply students must understand and exhibit their learning. Depth of learning is clearly described in Figure 3.4.

Depth of Learning	*Retention* of facts, terms, concepts, and the like are essential for further learning but do not require a deep level of understanding. This is reflected when students perform a portion of a musical piece that has been rehearsed.
	Comprehension is beyond knowledge retention and includes interpreting, compare and contrast, and explanation. For example, when a student has rehearsed multiple sections of a musical piece, the capacity to describe or demonstrate the differences between sections falls into this category.
	Application goes beyond demonstrating what has been rehearsed. This refers to applying knowledge and skills to new situations, much like problem solving. Sight-reading, for example, would be an excellent assessment at the level of application processing.
	Analysis is a process that requires deeper understanding, with the student recognizing and isolating compositional structures to successfully demonstrate learning through application. This includes identifying component parts of the composition and understanding the relationships that influence musical decisions and the principles behind the musical composition.
	Evaluation requires more depth of thinking through which the students judge the quality of music or performance based on criteria, logic, value, or usefulness.
	Creating is the highest level of processing, requiring students to synthesize all of the above and integrate ideas into a solution, action plan, or musical performance or improvise/compose an entirely new musical piece.

Figure 3.4 Considerations for depth of learning when writing objectives
Source: Adapted from Anderson & Krathwohl, 2001

Guidelines for Writing Learning Objectives

In contrast to broad goals of desired learning, and PLOs that are assessable components of learning goals, CLOs are specific measurable demonstrations of learning expected from a single course. CLOs contain the following three elements:

1. What is to be learned (knowledge, skill, disposition, or attitude)?
2. What level of learning is to be achieved (criteria, standard)?
3. Under what conditions is the learning to be demonstrated (environment, support, etc.)?

Stated in terms of what students do, learning objectives are stated with action verbs that clearly communicate the complexity of demonstration required of students. CLOs also must clarify expectations of quality. They should be sufficiently clear to guide teachers to develop appropriate assessment tasks through which students demonstrate their learning and for students to understand all expectations of learning.

In the process of writing clear course learning objectives, multiple revisions are often necessary to define and address learning expectations. Practical suggestions for developing learning objectives for music courses include (a) the ease of integration of assessments for learning

---

Learning Experience: Complete the following steps to develop PLOs and aligned CLOs:

STEP 1: Identify Programmatic Goals
Create a list of Program Learning Goals that encompass the categories of learning expected from students' involvement in courses across your program.
STEP 2: Define the Program Learning Outcomes (knowledge, skills, and dispositions/attitudes) encompassed in each goal you want students to display as a result of their overall educational and musical experience in your program.
Each goal typically consists of multiple component parts that are used by music educators to guide development of appropriate course instruction and assessments that indicate the level and quality of progress toward the PLO. • Define the components that will be used to guide the instructional focus within and across courses in your program. • Consider behavioral, cognitive, and affective constructs of learning and the standards of achievement expected for each category that will define your program.
STEP 3: Select one course for which to write Course Learning Objectives. • Consider how each PLO is reflected by the content and experiences taught in your class. • Each CLO is to be focused on how students will demonstrate their applied learning.
a) **Key Phrase:** The student will . . .
b) **Statement of the Desired Learning** (indicator of knowledge, skills or dispositions): This will probably be in the form of an action verb that describes what students will do to demonstrate learning. You might consider the levels of complexity according to Bloom's Taxonomy.
c) **Statement about conditions:** Identify under what circumstances, or in what environment, the student will be expected to demonstrate their learning?
d) **Statement about expected rigor:** At what level of achievement and what criteria defines the expectation for the objective?

objectives, (b) the measurability of the defined learning, (c) appropriateness for student development and achievement, and (d) external expectations for which students must prepare (e.g., festival or college placement auditions).

As curricula evolve, it is also important to recognize that CLOs may change over time to address current course expectations or changing characteristics of students, but the PLOs will most likely remain the same. Three guiding principles frame the review of existing learning objectives: *recency*: the degree to which the objectives reflect current knowledge and practice expected in a program; *relevance*: the degree to which the objectives relate logically and significantly to course intentions; and *rigor*: the degree of musical precision and depth required for the outcome to be met successfully. These three factors, once clearly defined, are the foundation for lesson planning and designing instructional activities and student learning assessments.

Selected Assessments

Although discussed more thoroughly later, it is appropriate to discuss relevant terminology and constructs associated with the assessments tasks through which students demonstrate the CLOs. There are two overarching forms of assessments, *direct* and *indirect*. **Direct assessments** are measures of student learning through which students demonstrate the quality of achievement and how they transfer their learning to an applied setting. **Indirect assessments** tend to measure perceptions and opinions of student learning and how this learning is valued. These forms of assessment are often external to music coursework and music program curricula. It is also possible to assess beliefs directly. See Table 3.1 for a few examples of each.

Measurement in assessment refers to the process that derives information about the quality of student learning. A measuring device must break down the objectives into specific characteristics, traits, or criteria. Since no one assessment task can fully address all aspects of music learning and students generally do not demonstrate their full capacity of learning at any one assessment event, assessment experts suggest the use of multiple and varied assessments across time for each learning objective. It is also important to consider that students can demonstrate learning in multiple ways depending upon the depth of understanding or skill and the student's personal goals. For this reason, it is important to corroborate and/or triangulate the assessment results with consideration of an established standard of performance for each trait. This means compare findings from multiple assessments to (a) identify whether they illustrate a similar conclusion about student learning and (b) expose indications of learning not evident in all

Table 3.1 Examples of direct and indirect assessments

Content: Knowledge of subject matter	**Examples of direct assessments:** • Musical vocabulary tests • Portfolios • Essays/reports of musical composers, styles, or pieces • Oral reports • Program notes • Website development • Performance self-analysis • Peer feedback
Skill acquisition: Application of musical constructs, demonstration of a competency, etc.	**Examples of direct assessments:** • Performance test • Scored solo/ensemble performance • Sectional leadership • Sight-reading • Compositions/improvisations
Attitudes: Awareness, interest, concern, etc. (affective learning)	**Examples of direct assessments:** • Observation of intended action and decisions reflecting students' attitudes • Stated goal and intentions for future accomplishment • Demonstrated initiative, attitudes, or application of beliefs
Knowledge, Skills, and Attitudes:	**Examples of indirect assessments:** • Student self-evaluation of their learning and/or achievement • Survey of students' attitudes • Opinions of external observers

assessments. For example, to identify the capability of accurately reading musical notation, you could ask a student to perform a segment from a piece in their ensemble music folder. But the findings from this assessment task should be corroborated with findings from other assessments such as sight-reading a segment of similar difficulty and complexity, as well as performing technical passages or exercises. Triangulation literally means taking three or more assessment findings associated with the same learning objective and evaluating all to determine the extent to which the student demonstrates the expected learning. Through corroboration and triangulation of evidence, a music teacher can expose aspects of learning and achievement beyond what is capable with a single assessment. There are many ways to measure learning objectives and outcomes, and these will be discussed in Chapters 4 and 6. Of primary consideration is to reflect how students authentically demonstrate their learning in a fair and applicable assessment situation. Thorough assessment is the responsibility of all music teachers, and effective CLO assessment becomes informative to understanding programmatic effectiveness through assessment reporting.

Other Considerations

A common term used in music is authentic assessment (see Chapter 6). This refers to assessment tasks that reflect what and how musicians experience music beyond the classroom setting in real-world situations. Asking for students to authentically demonstrate music learning in an applied setting is common in a school music classroom. Some assessment practices within a program are questionable, however, in reference to authenticity. For example, it is common for students to learn to perform within an ensemble setting, but an assessment task that requires students to perform individually in an office or on a recording device is outside of the experienced context. This new context differs from the authentic learning context and may not produce information that authentically reflects the performance quality of the student. In many cases, the new context adds layers of discomfort that could easily alter the quality of student performance during an assessment. It is important for students to develop comfort with demonstrating their learning in the same context in which they will be assessed. Another example of a questionable assessment practice sometimes administered in a school setting is in the area of music reading skills. If an assessment task is to score students' performance on well-rehearsed passage, one must question whether their reading skill is authentically assessed. Repetition can often lead to automaticity of technical skills overriding the skill of music reading. Authentic assessments should be designed for students to demonstrate learning in the context in which the expected outcome is learned and applied. To measure how well a student reads notation, a notation test may be more authentic, but if the intention is to measure how well a student can perform notation, a sight-reading playing test may be the most authentic.

Assessment can also be designed for what is sometimes referred to as a "growth model." Federal and state priorities required that student growth measures be taken in an attempt to indicate teacher quality (Goe & Holdheide, 2011), and it was proposed that measuring growth was a fairer way to assess teacher quality for those who worked in schools whose students were considerably behind their peers in other schools in proficiency. This structure of assessment is designed to measure changes in student learning and/or achievement across time. This purpose of assessment requires at least two measurements, one prior and one following the learning experience. If assessment tasks and measures used in both instances are at the same level of difficulty and reflect similar complexity, then the scores can be compared to identify progress in learning; however, the challenge with growth assessment is that instruction increases across time in difficulty and/or complexity. When we assess students at two points in time, it is a common and desirable practice to adjust the assessment instrument to reflect the intended progress. When assessments then become increasingly challenging, the scores may not effectively demonstrate growth.

An additional problem with pre- and post-testing is that an improvement score does not necessarily confirm whether a student meets acceptable levels of achievement. For example, if a student begins at a low level of achievement and shows a high range of improvement, this does not mean that this particular student has reached the expected level of achievement. It only shows that they improved on the measure used. Conversely, a student who began at a high level of proficiency and then exceeds grade-level expectations may not show a wide range of improvement but has demonstrated meeting and exceeding expectations. Thus, an assessment process based primarily on growth/progress is problematic for identifying whether desired expectations or standards of achievement have been met.

Regardless of whether growth is observed or the objectives set have been achieved, all assessment tasks have the capacity to be **formative**: that is, the assessment findings can be used to inform instructional decisions, provide feedback to the students on achievement, or be used as a baseline for future learning goals. The formative nature of assessment is a very important component of the teaching and learning process. Assessment tasks can also be used to measure a particular level of achievement at specified time in the learning process (e.g., the end of a unit); the measure becomes **summative**.

Summary

Assessments that occur within courses can be useful in identifying the effectiveness of a music program's curricular sequence, content, and impact on student achievement. By establishing a matrix of how PLOs are taught and assessed across courses, a timeline for collecting selected evidence of student achievement from coursework (CLOs), and a plan to review and analyze data on student learning pertaining to the PLOs, then the program can make determinations as to the curricular effectiveness, effectiveness of instructional practice, and development of student learning across the program. This all fits into a teaching, learning, and assessment process that begins with defining learning outcomes and the assessments through which students will demonstrate achievement. These are used to guide instructional/curricular decisions and planning (see Figure 3.5).

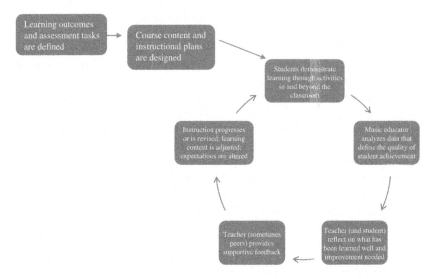

Figure 3.5 Teaching, learning, and assessment process

References

Anderson, L., & Krathwohl, D. (2001). *A taxonomy for learning, teaching, and assessing: A revision of Bloom's Taxonomy of Educational Objectives.* New York, NY: Longman.

Bernard, C. F., & Abramo, J. M. (2019). *Teacher evaluation in music.* New York, NY: Oxford University Press.

Fautley, M. (2010). *Assessment in music education.* New York, NY: Oxford University Press.

Goe, L., & Holdheide, L. (2011). *Measuring teachers' contributions to student learning growth for nontested grades and subjects.* Research and Policy Brief, National Comprehensive Center for Teacher Quality. Retrieved from https://files.eric.ed.gov/fulltext/ED520722.pdf

Lehman, P. (1992). Assessing learning in the music classroom. *NASSP Bulletin,* 76(544), 56–62. http://hdl.handle.net/2027.42/67410

Martell, K. (2005). Overcoming faculty resistance to assessment. In K. Martell & C. T. Calderon (Eds.), *Assessment of student learning in business schools: Best practices each step of the way* (Vol. 1(2), pp. 210–226). Tallahassee, FL: The Association for Institutional Research.

Popham, W. J. (2003). *Test better, teach better: The instructional role of assessment.* Alexandria, VA: Association for Supervision and Curriculum Development.

Learning Experience

Overall Program Learning Goals

Using the information from the earlier experience, create a set of five overall student learning goals that can apply to all levels/courses of a music program. These are broad goals that will be adapted for all courses and student developmental levels.

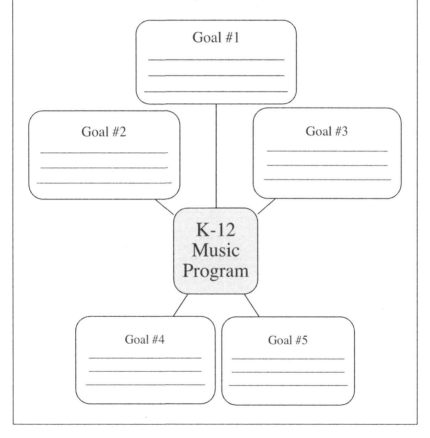

Goal #1

Goal #2

Goal #3

K-12 Music Program

Goal #4

Goal #5

Learning Experience

PLOs

For each broad learning goal, define two specific program outcomes that can apply to any course or student achievement level.

Program Goal #1

Program Goal #2

Program Goal #3

Program Goal #4

Program Goal #5

Learning Experience

CLOs

Write CLOs that can be used on a course syllabus.

- *Clearly defined student learning objectives.*
- *Identify instructional assessment tasks.*
- *Define measures to expose qualities of student learning.*

Structure for objectives *(e.g., "The students will (desired behavior) (conditions) (expected rigor)."*

Course _____

Learning Objectives for the Course	Instructional task that could be used to assess student learning	How will student learning be measured

Learning Experience

Developmentally Sequencing PLOs Within CLOs

Develop a structure that aligns five goals, component outcomes, and course objectives across grade levels and courses in a school music program.

School Music Program						
Program Goals	Program Learning Outcomes	Grades 1-2 CLO	Grades 3-4 CLO	Grades 5-6 CLO	Grades 7-8 CLO	Grades 9-12 CLO
	1.					
	2.					
	1.					
	2.					
	1.					
	2.					
	1.					
	2.					
	1.					
	2.					

4 Developing Learning Outcomes, Assessment Tasks, and Scoring Devices

Brian C. Wesolowski and Phillip Payne

Chapter Overview

This chapter is designed to describe the processes by which music educators can develop student-learning **outcomes**, align assessment tasks with stated outcomes, and create scoring devices to collect data within a teaching unit in order to provide detailed, timely, and meaningful feedback and analysis for both students and educators.

Learning Expectations for the Chapter

- Describe the usefulness of educational taxonomies in the context of music assessment.
- Choose and craft learning outcomes appropriate for various grade levels and music learning contexts.
- Develop an assessment blueprint aligned to a learning outcome.
- Develop a table of specifications aligned to a test.

Essential Questions for the Chapter

- What are some important educational taxonomies and how can they be used effectively to guide and facilitate assessment practices?
- What are the components to a learning outcome and what part do they play in the assessment context?
- How can an assessment blueprint help facilitate instruction related to a learning outcome?
- How can a table of specifications provide evidence of content validity and support assessment processes?

Introduction

Over the course of the past half-century, the focus of educational quality has shifted from an educator-centered focus to a learner-centered focus. The foundation of this shift was grounded in the concept that learning takes place within the student. According to Fink (2003), if no change is observed within the student, than no learning has taken place. Therefore, centering efforts on developing instruction to deliver content evolved into developing instruction aligned with specific student-learning outcomes. Clearly articulating student-learning outcomes establishes transparency between the student and educator regarding what the student is expected to demonstrate upon completion of a lesson, unit, course, or program. This chapter focuses on teaching units, at the individual lesson level, and is designed to describe the process by which educators can develop student-learning outcomes, align assessment tasks with stated outcomes, and create scoring devices to collect data as a method for improving the teaching and learning processes. Combined, this process can enhance the clarity and quality of instruction within the music classroom while also allowing for a more rigorous and effective evaluation of student learning.

Educational Taxonomies

A common method for describing and facilitating the discussion regarding learning processes is through the use of **educational taxonomies**. Merriam-Webster defines a taxonomy as the "general principles of scientific classification" (Merriam-Webster Online Dictionary, n.d.). In the case of educational taxonomies, many researchers have classified learning through a series of sequential lenses. Educational taxonomies are often used to describe *levels* of learning taking place within the classroom. There are several educational taxonomies/frameworks that have emerged within the educational literature that are designed in a hierarchical manner. Examples of these include the Taxonomy of Educational Objectives (Bloom, 1956), the Revised Bloom's Taxonomy of Educational Objectives (Anderson & Krathwohl, 2001), the Structure of Observed Learning Outcomes (SOLO) taxonomy (Biggs & Collis, 1982), the Gagné Taxonomy (Gagné, 1965; Gagné & Briggs, 1974), the Ausubel and Robinson Taxonomy (Ausubel & Robinson, 1969), the New Taxonomy of Educational Objectives (Marzano & Kendall, 2007), and Webb's Depth of Knowledge Framework (Webb, 1997). For the sake of brevity and clarity, this chapter focuses on three of the more common taxonomies currently used in today's educational landscape as a reference for developing and hierarchically structuring learning objectives: (a) Bloom's Taxonomy of Educational Objectives (Bloom, 1956),

(b) the Revised Bloom's Taxonomy of Educational Objectives (Anderson & Krathwohl, 2001), and (c) the SOLO taxonomy (Biggs & Collis, 1982).

Bloom's Taxonomy of Educational Objectives

Benjamin Bloom (University of Chicago), along with collaborators Max Englehart, Edward Furst, Walter Hill, and David Krathwohl, developed Bloom's Taxonomy of Educational Objectives (1956). This framework is designed in a hierarchical nature that consists of three domains each divided into several categories sequenced from simple to complex. The three domains include the cognitive domain, psychomotor domain, and affective domain.

The **cognitive domain** is divided into six categories sequenced from simple cognitive tasks to more complex cognitive tasks: (a) knowledge, (b) comprehension, (c) application, (d) analysis, (e) synthesis, and (f) creation (see Figure 4.1). The following are some brief explanations of each of the six categories (Bloom, 1956, pp. 201–207):

1. **Knowledge.** The *knowledge* level includes students' abilities to recall specifics and universals, methods and processes, or patterns, structures, or settings (e.g., Students will be able to recognize, recall, identify).
2. **Comprehension.** The *comprehension* level includes students' abilities to understand such that they know what is being communicated and can make use of the material or idea being communicated without necessarily relating it to other material or seeing its fullest implications (e.g., Students will be able to associate, explain, generalize).
3. **Application.** The *application* level includes students' abilities to use abstractions in particular and concrete situations (e.g., Students will be able to classify, graph, modify).
4. **Analysis.** The *analysis* level includes students' abilities to break down communication into its constituent elements or parts such that the relative hierarchy of ideas is made clear and/or the relations between ideas expressed are made explicit (e.g., Students will be able to differentiate, outline, relate).
5. **Synthesis.** The *synthesis* level includes students' abilities to put together elements and parts so as to form a whole (e.g., Students will be able to generate, reconstruct, rewrite).
6. **Evaluation.** The *evaluation* level includes students' judgments about the value of material and methods for given purposes (e.g., Students will be able to contrast, grade, rank).

Figure 4.1 Bloom's original cognitive domain

Revised Bloom's Taxonomy of Educational Objectives

In 2001, a group of researchers updated Bloom's original taxonomy to account for new research and development within the profession (Anderson & Krathwohl, 2001). In their revision, they converted the category descriptors from nouns to verbs to better reflect the learning process as experienced by the students. Furthermore, it positioned the student to be more active within the learning process and included two reimagined categories, Evaluate and Create. The researchers felt that the process of creation was more complex than synthesizing already known information. They also provide clearer indications of expectations within each category (Anderson & Krathwohl, 2001). The six revised categories (see Figure 4.2) include:

1. **Remember**. The *remember* level includes students' abilities to recall information such as dates, events, places, ideas, definitions, or theories (e.g., Students will be able to recognize, recall, identify).
2. **Understand**. The *understand* level includes students' abilities to grasp meaning of the information, express it in their own words, and cite examples (e.g., Students will be able to associate, explain, generalize).
3. **Apply**. The *apply* level includes students' abilities to apply knowledge or skills to new situations, use information and knowledge to solve a problem, answer a question, or perform another task (e.g., Students will be able to classify, graph, modify).

Figure 4.2 Revised categories of Bloom's cognitive domain

4. **Analyze.** The *analyze* level includes students' abilities to break down knowledge into parts and show and explain the relationships among the parts (e.g., Students will be able to differentiate, outline, relate).
5. **Evaluate.** The *evaluate* level includes students' abilities to judge or assess the value of material and methods for a given purpose (e.g., Students will be able to contrast, grade, rank).
6. **Create.** The *create* level includes the students' abilities to pull together parts of knowledge to form a new whole and build relationships for new situations (e.g., Students will be able to generate, reconstruct, rewrite).

Beyond the cognitive domain, there are two other domains that are equally appropriate to music education. These domains are the psychomotor domain and affective domain. Similar to the cognitive domain, the psychomotor and affective domains are divided into categories from simple tasks to more complex tasks. The **psychomotor domain**[1] (Dave, 1970) includes physical movement, coordination, and the use of fine motor skills. Development at each level is based upon speed, precision, procedures, and technique, all of which require practice and attention to detail (see Figure 4.3). Tasks can range from breathing to complex finger patterns to performing while moving (e.g., marching band or show choir). The psychomotor domain is divided into seven categories:

1. **Perception.** The *perception* level includes the students' abilities to use sensory clues to guide motor activity (e.g., Students will be able to choose, describe, detect, isolate).
2. **Set.** The *set* level includes the students' readiness to act (e.g., Students will be able to display, explain, react, demonstrate).
3. **Guided response.** The *guided response* level includes the students' abilities related to rote learning and guided practice (e.g., Students will be able to copy, reproduce, respond).
4. **Mechanism.** The *mechanism* level includes the students' development of performance habits (e.g., Students will be able to fix manipulate, organize, sketch).
5. **Complex overt response.** The *complex overt response* level describes the students' efficiency of technique (e.g., Same as mechanism, but students demonstrate more efficiency and faster speed).

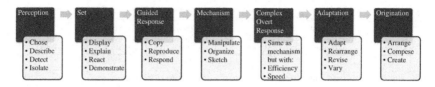

Figure 4.3 Psychomotor domain

6. **Adaptation.** The *adaptation* level includes the students' abilities to transfer or modify technique to fit a specific situation e.g., Students will be able to adapt, rearrange, revise, vary).
7. **Origination.** The *origination* level includes the students' abilities to establish new techniques to make current study more efficient (e.g., Students will be able to arrange, compose, create).

The **affective domain,** first introduced by Krathwohl, Bloom, and Masia (1964), is a framework that organizes the process by which students confront issues within their daily lives. The learner evolves from learning a concept, to an awareness of learning that concept, and finally into internalizing the concept in a way that aids in guiding all future actions. This is especially important within music education as it establishes aesthetic value while internalizing the act of making music. Furthermore, addressing the affective domain promotes a deeper level of self-knowledge through the impact on future actions (see Figure 4.4). Among the areas covered by the affective domain are (a) feelings, (b) values, (c) emotions, (d) appreciation, (e) motivations, and (f) attitudes. The affective domain is split into five categories:

1. **Receiving phenomena.** The *receiving phenomena* level includes students' awareness of surrounding stimuli and observants (e.g., *acknowledge, listens, attentive*).
2. **Responds to phenomena.** The *responds to phenomena* level includes students' attention and specific reactions to given stimuli (e.g., *assists, conforms, presents*).
3. **Valuing.** The *valuing* level includes the worth students attach to a specific entity, object, or experience (e.g., *appreciates, justifies, respects*).
4. **Organization.** The *organization* level includes students' priority of values through comparing and synthesis (e.g., *compares, relates, synthesizes*).
5. **Characterization.** The *characterization* level includes students' abilities to establish a value system that informs their behaviors and decision-making (e.g., *displays, modifies, solves*).

Figure 4.4 Affective domain

The three domains of Bloom's Taxonomies align well with the 2014 National Core Arts Standards of *Create*, *Perform*, and *Respond*. Furthermore, focusing on musical content knowledge (i.e., cognitive domain), skills (i.e., psychomotor domain), and dispositions (i.e., affective domain) can serve as a formidable foundation for learning outcomes across a program, course, unit, or lesson. Throughout the early stages of composing student learning outcomes, consulting Bloom's Taxonomy of Educational Objectives and Revised Bloom's Taxonomy may provide a strong, foundational starting point.

The SOLO Taxonomy

The SOLO (Biggs & Collis, 1982) taxonomy is diverse in its inclusion of various content and focuses more on the development of structural complexity across abilities of the learner. Additionally, each level of the taxonomy contains similar stages across a variety of tasks (Hook & Mills, 2011). According to Biggs and Collis, students' understanding increases in complexity within a variety of subjects through a series of five levels (see Figure 4.5). The five levels include:

1. **Pre-structural.** In the *pre-structural* level, students are unsure about the lesson and they are simplistic in their approach to the concept (e.g., Students fail, are incompetent, or miss the point).
2. **Uni-structural.** In the *uni-structural* level, students are solely focused on one component of a given concept (e.g., Students will be able to identify, name, follow instructions, recall).
3. **Multi-structural.** In the *multi-structural* level, students successfully internalize and engage in multiple independent components within a given concept (e.g., Students will be able to combine, describe, perform, list).
4. **Relational.** In the *relational* level, students demonstrate a global understanding of a concept by synthesizing the all of the provided concepts into one coherent structure (e.g., Students will be able to analyze, apply, compare/contrast, relate, justify, support, critique).
5. **Extended abstract.** In the *extended abstract* level, students generalize newly internalized conceptual structures to new areas based on their newly attained mastery (e.g., Students will be able to create, generate, reflect, hypothesize).

Figure 4.5 The SOLO taxonomy

Supporters of the SOLO taxonomy suggest there are many advantages to designing instruction and courses around these processes. These advantages are in item construction and scoring, more connection to the progression of both student learning and teaching, and most notably that the levels can be applied relative to the development of the student (Hook & Mills, 2011). For instance, a seventh-grade trombone player could be asked to generate melodic ideas for a possible improvisation at a different level of abstraction compared to a college sophomore counterpart. Finally, proponents of the SOLO taxonomy suggest that it is easier to identify, categorize, and create tests through implementation of this framework.

Taxonomies and Their Impact on Music Learning

Payne, Burrack, Parkes, and Wesolowski (2019) describe the emerging process of assessment in music education. They share a process that reflects a cycle of measuring the knowledge and skills of young musicians in school music programs. Within this process is identifying the difficulty and complexity levels at which the students are performing. Given the 2014 National Core Arts Music Standards, students are expected to demonstrate all levels of complexity on a multitude of difficulty levels. Create, Perform, and Respond (processes) fit well within all of the above-mentioned taxonomies. It is the music educator's task to decide which taxonomy best reflects their philosophy of education as well as their beliefs about how students best learn and interact with music. While individual school districts may subscribe to one or the other, being aware of how they coexist and relate to each other is paramount. Consistency in application of these taxonomies is critical for defining, constructing, and implementing a robust and effective assessment protocol within a music program and related curricula.

In regard to Bloom's Taxonomy of Educational Objectives, all three domains are useful within the music program. The emergence of the psychomotor and affective domain alongside the often-cited cognitive domain is essential for music education. Music educators are often focused on developing complete musicians within their programs, which requires more than just the mental perspective of music making. Each day, students are asked to breathe differently, make sounds differently, interpret music, decode gestures, internalize pulse, and perform many other tasks. Unfortunately, these tasks cannot all be evaluated using the cognitive domain alone. Unlocking the door to the psychomotor and affective domains may be transformational in improving student achievement.

As an example, consider the use of the psychomotor domain for the evaluation of student ability in a beginning band. When a beginning-band instructor is working with young students on new instruments, how can a learning **objective** be written beyond the focus of music reading? Perhaps using learning objectives focused on technique, dexterity, and finger patterns, among others, would be useful to measure and articulate a holistic picture of student learning.

As another example, consider the use of the affective domain for the evaluation of a student's feelingful response to the music performed in an intermediate orchestra. When an intermediate-orchestra conductor is developing musicianship within her program, consider how she could appropriately measure the affective connection of her students to the repertoire. What dispositions could be demonstrated by students that could be measured for connection to the music and students' musicality? The affective domain provides a taxonomy to better define these interactions. O'Toole (2003) notes that educators are often not accustomed to writing these types of learning goals because they are typically difficult to articulate and/or define. Furthermore, they are often long-term in nature and develop slowly throughout experiences within music programs.

Music education assessment can be effectively contextualized through a music educator's implementation of the SOLO taxonomy. Music is not unidimensional. Students must develop knowledge, skills, abilities, and dispositions across a variety of concepts and structures. The strength of this framework is its flexibility. The SOLO taxonomy can allow for varying abilities of learners to operate at high levels of complexity simultaneously. This will allow the music educator to differentiate instruction through well-designed assessments to meet each student at their current developmental level. This is most applicable in large high school non-auditioned ensembles where there is a wide variety of ability levels and engagement in the content. Furthermore, the SOLO taxonomy may also help expose potential teaching opportunities for the educator.

Given these taxonomies, there are several implications for music education assessment. Each has a connection to music and should be considered when crafting learning objectives for the music classroom. As a music educator, it is important to consider one's music philosophy toward the most appropriate approach and to remain consistent through the assessment design process.

Crafting Learning Objectives

The ability of an educator to write learning objectives is one of the most critical components of assessment in the music classroom. Without a measurable learning objective, developing **valid, reliable,** and **fair** assessments

is not possible. Furthermore, well-defined, measurable objectives establish a foundation of effective advocacy of your music education program
(Payne et al., 2019). Mager (1984) identified three foundational components of learning objectives: (a) conditions, (b) a performance or action
verb (i.e., an observable behavior), and (c) criteria. Identifying and labeling
each section ensures an effective, specific, and measurable outcome. When
writing objectives, the first step is to start with the end in mind. Envision a
student's final demonstration of a student-learning outcome. What should
students to be able to do at the end of instruction? What behaviors or
tasks should they demonstrate? Where and for whom will they perform
these tasks? To what level will they perform? These guiding questions will
provide the foundation for creating measurable learning outcomes.

Conditions

Conditions refer to the situation or context of the learners. This can vary
from time limits (e.g., end of class, end of the course, end of the instructional cycle) to ensemble type or any descriptor that provides a context of
the situation of the learners. Establishing the conditions allows for more
detailed analysis and connection with learning because of the context.

> Ex. 1.1 Original: Students will be able to sing through *Loch
> Lomond* . . .
> Ex. 1.1 Revised: <u>*By the end of the unit*</u>, students will perform *Loch
> Lomond* . . .
> Ex. 1.1 Revised: <u>*Given a model*</u>, students will match Scottish vowels
> in *Loch Lomond* . . .

As indicated in the examples above, conditions refer to what the students
are provided to successfully complete a task or a time frame in which the
task should be completed. These conditions are critical in establishing
incremental learning goals leading to meeting course, unit, or program
outcomes. When educators clearly define the conditions, it provides them
an opportunity to accurately measure, document, communicate, and
respond to student learning in a timely and meaningful way.

Within the conditions, both the learning environment and intended
learners should also be a focus of consideration. Descriptors of the audience (i.e., the context and learners) can often be included in the conditions.
Who is your intended audience? What are their general characteristics?
What are their learning styles? If educators do not have answers to these
questions, then any objective written will not yield data that will be effective in assessment.

> Ex. 1.2 Original: By the end of <u>*class*</u>, the students will . . .
> Ex. 1.2 Revised: By the end of <u>*beginning woodwinds class*</u>, the
> students will . . .

In the example above, specifying the audience as a beginning woodwinds class clearly defines the intended learners and their level of development. Addressing consistent embouchure, constant work on establishing a characteristic tone, developing basic finger patterns, maintaining a consistent air stream, and connecting sounds to music reading skills are among some considerations that will guide the development of outcomes, assessments, and expectations. Defining the audience allows the educator to write learning outcomes and establish criteria to aid in both student learning and growth.

Action Verb (Observable Behavior)

The *action verb* specifies the way students are expected to demonstrate learning. This component involves, and is sometimes referred to as, a measurable, observable *behavior*.[2] Students must be engaged in authentic learning and *actively doing* something. The educator should clearly define what the students are doing by selecting an action verb that focuses on meeting the learning objective as well as the level of complexity. For instance, if an educator chooses the word *compose*, then it can be assumed that higher-level thinking skills are required as creation of new content requires a higher level of cognition than recall. While writing objectives, avoiding passive verbs, connections to ability, or vague descriptors such as *understand* and *perform*.[3] Precisely what the students will do is critical.

> Ex. 1.3 Original: Students will *understand compositional techniques* of *Kingfishers Catch Fire*.
> Ex. 1.3 Revised: Students will *compose a 16-bar rhythm track* to accompany warm-ups using a given chord progression and a minimum of two rhythms from *Kingfishers Catch Fire*.

Criteria

Criteria , or *degree of mastery*, define the specific change in behavior that is sought by the instructor. To what extent will students demonstrate the specified change in behavior? Criteria can be described and measured in a variety of ways, including ordinal expectations, number of mistakes allowable, and percentage of passing. The educator determines the threshold of acceptance (and in some cases mastery) to set the performance standard. These thresholds will change based upon piloting of assessments or constant review of collected data and student performance. Criteria can then be set for varying levels to provide specific and differentiated feedback for a variety of levels of students within the music classroom.

> Ex. 1.4 Original: Students will be able to *successfully perform* Line 75.
> Ex. 1.4 Revised: By the end of the lesson, students will demonstrate Line 75 *with fewer than two mistakes in pulse or duration*.

In Ex. 1.4, the educator does not have a clear definition of "successfully"; therefore, it is difficult to indicate when a student has completed Line 75. However, in the revision of Ex. 1.4, the educator has identified pulse and duration as the main focus of this exercise and it is clear as to the expectation of the student and the level to which they are expected to demonstrate the musical example.

Checking the Quality of Objective Writing

Since objective writing is the critical first step in assessment, quality control is paramount. Below are some tips and guiding questions to ensure that you have the most specific, measurable, and effective learning outcomes and objectives:

- *Three parts*. Have the conditions, action verb, and criteria been identified?
- *Use action verbs*. Students are active in the learning process. Connect these action verbs to taxonomies that connect with levels of cognition, psychomotor, and the affective domains. Ensure that a balance of levels within these taxonomies is obvious.
- *Is it measurable?* Are intended outcomes composed of clear and measurable components and actions?
- *Be succinct*. Precision is paramount in creating specific, measurable, and effective learning objectives.
- *Be specific*. Vagueness in verb choice is problematic in designing useful assessments. Avoid verbs like "understand" or passive verbs. Instead, describe what knowledge and skills a student must master in order to gain an understanding of a concept.
- *Student-focused*. All objectives should be centered on student learning.
- *SMART*. This acronym will refine objectives further. Do objectives meet the following criteria: S-pecific, M-easurable, A-cceptable, R-ealistic, and T-imebound?[4]
- *Consult given curriculum*. Learning objectives should emerge from course and curricular goals and outcomes. Be sure that objectives are aligned with a curriculum as well as instructional and assessment activities.

Preplanning Assessment Processes

It is important for educators to plan assessment processes prior to instruction in order to ensure valid, reliable, and fair inferences of student learning. As will be described in Chapter 5, there are several considerations for **validity**, **reliability**, and **fairness** in the context of the music classroom.

Many of these considerations can be considered during the preplanning stages of classroom assessment processes:

- *Relevance of testing*. The preplanning of classroom assessment processes ensures that educators are aligning the content covered within the assessment task to national/state standards, the content taught throughout the instructional unit, and detailed learning outcomes of the instructional unit.
- *Levels of thinking processes*. The preplanning of classroom assessment processes ensures that multiple levels of a selected educational taxonomy are addressed, specifically targeting the students' abilities.
- *Differentiation of assessment types*. The preplanning of classroom assessment processes ensures that information about students' knowledge, skills, abilities, or dispositions being tested are collected through differentiated assessment types utilizing multiple scoring tools.
- *Clear communication of expectations*. The preplanning of classroom assessment processes ensures that expectations, outcomes, and uses of the test are provided to students prior to instruction, thereby communicating learning outcome expectations.
- *Transparency*. The preplanning of classroom assessment processes ensures that students have not only a clear interpretation of assessment expectations but also clarity regarding the purpose of the test as well as any related consequences of the assessment process.
- *Student opportunities*. The preplanning of classroom assessment processes ensures that students will have the opportunity to demonstrate their acquired knowledge, skills, abilities, and/or dispositions through differentiation of assessment types.

Assessment Blueprints and Tables of Specification

The terms *assessment blueprint*, *test blueprint*, and *table of specifications* are often used interchangeably throughout various instructional texts and research literature in the field of applied educational assessment. The following sections will deliberately draw a distinction between an *assessment blueprint* and a *table of specifications* as two important, but separate, tools for planning and implementing testing processes suited for the music classroom.

Developing an Assessment Blueprint

An **assessment blueprint** is a concise plan of action that captures the multiple methods in which an educator intends to formally test students' academic performance in the classroom within a given instructional unit. The assessment blueprint serves as a method for preplanning how the educator will capture and evaluate the multiple streams of knowledge, skills, abilities, and/or dispositions students demonstrate aligned to expected learning outcomes. The same way educators use lesson plans to plan, guide, and facilitate instruction in the classroom, educators can use assessment blueprints to plan, guide, and facilitate evaluative processes within the classroom.

The exemplar assessment blueprint in this chapter is based upon the structure of the National Core Arts Music Standards (2014). However, it may be adapted to fit any structure most suitable for the policies or practices specific to the educator's state or district. In the example described below, there are many possible methods for assessing the intended learning outcomes of the sample instructional unit. *The focus in this example should not necessarily be the chosen objectives and methods; rather, the focus should be on the documentation methods for the assessment blueprint.*

Figure 4.6 is a sample assessment blueprint that documents all of the artistic processes, artistic process components, anchor standards, and

Author:	John Davidson		
Music Program:	Lincoln Middle School Band Program		
Class:	7th grade Intermediate Band		
Instructional Unit:	Rhythm Identification and Performance for quarter note/eighth note combinations		
All Artistic Process(es) to Be Assessed:	All Artistic Process Component(s) to Be Assessed:	Anchor Standard(s) to Be Assessed:	
Performing	Analyze Present	Analyze the structure and context of varied musical works and their implications for performance. Perform expressively, with appropriate interpretation and technical accuracy, and in a manner appropriate to the audience and context.	
Performance Standard(s):			
MU:Pr4.2.E.5a Demonstrate, using music reading skills where appropriate, how knowledge of formal aspects in musical works inform prepared or improvised performances. MU:Pr6.1.E.5a Demonstrate attention to technical accuracy and expressive qualities in prepared and improvised performances of a varied repertoire of music.			
ASSESSMENT 1			
Purpose of the Assessment	Students will and visually identify rhythmic structures found in the music repertoire.		
Enduring Understanding(s)	Analyzing creators' context and how they manipulate elements of music provides insight into their intent and informs performance.		
Essential Question(s)	How does understanding the structure and context of musical works inform performance?		
Performance Standard(s)	Anchor Standard	Artistic Process Component	Artistic Process
MU:Pr4.2.E.5a Demonstrate, using music reading skills where appropriate, how knowledge of formal aspects in musical works inform prepared or improvised performances.	Analyze	Analyze the structure and context of varied musical works and their implications for performance.	Perform
Scoring Device Name(s):	Rhythm Identification Test		
Type of Scoring Device(s):	True and False Multiple Choice Fill in the Blank		
Student Task(s):	Selected Response		
Item/Criteria Type(s):			

Figure 4.6 Sample assessment blueprint

ASSESSMENT 2			
Purpose of the Assessment	Students will perform rhythmic structures found in the music repertoire in the context of a sight-reading test.		
Enduring Understanding(s)	Musicians judge performance based on criteria that vary across time, place, and cultures. The context and how a work is presented influence the audience response.		
Essential Question(s)	When is a performance judged ready to present? How do context and the manner in which musical work is presented influence audience response?		
Performance Standard(s)	Anchor Standard	Artistic Process Component	Artistic Process
MU:Pr6.1.E.5a Demonstrate attention to technical accuracy and expressive qualities in prepared and improvised performances of a varied repertoire of music.	Present	Perform expressively, with appropriate interpretation and technical accuracy, and in a manner appropriate to the audience and context.	Perform
Scoring Device Name:	Model Cornerstone Assessment: Performance Evaluation (Novice)		
Type of Scoring Device(s):	Rubric		
Student Task(s):	Performance Task		
Item/Criteria Type(s):	1. Rhythm and Pulse Accuracy		
ASSESSMENT 3			
Purpose of the Assessment	Students will perform rhythmic structures found in the music repertoire in the context of the music literature.		
Enduring Understanding	Musicians judge performance based on criteria that vary across time, place, and cultures. The context and how a work is presented influence the audience response.		
Essential Question	When is a performance judged ready to present? How do context and the manner in which musical work is presented influence audience response?		
Performance Standard(s)	Anchor Standard	Artistic Process Component	Artistic Process
Demonstrate attention to technical accuracy and expressive qualities in prepared and improvised performances of a varied repertoire of music.	Present	Perform expressively, with appropriate interpretation and technical accuracy, and in a manner appropriate to the audience and context.	Perform
Scoring Device Name:	Model Cornerstone Assessment: Performance Evaluation (Novice)		
Type of Scoring Device(s):	Rubric		
Student Tasks (s):	Performance Task		
Item/Criteria Type(s):	1. Tone Production 2. Rhythm and Pulse Accuracy 3. Pitch and Intonation Accuracy 4. Expressive Qualities/Stylistic Interpretation		

Figure 4.6 Continued

performance standards assessed in a given instructional unit as well as information specific to each of the scoring devices used. The salient features of the assessment blueprint include:

- *Artistic Processes:* Artistic processes are the cognitive and physical actions by which arts learning and making are realized (National Coalition of Core Arts Standards, 2014). Outside of the context of the National Core Arts Standards, performance standards are commonly referred to as global objectives (Wesolowski, 2015).
- *Artistic Process Components:* Artistic process components are the actions artists carry out as they complete each artistic process

(National Coalition of Core Arts Standards, 2014). Outside of the context of the National Core Arts Standards, anchor standards are commonly referred to as educational objectives (Wesolowski, 2015).

- *Anchor Standards:* Anchor standards describe the general knowledge and skill that educators expect students to demonstrate throughout their education in the arts (National Coalition of Core Arts Standards, 2014). Anchor standards are associated with the verbs embedded within educational taxonomies and provide information related to the cognitive, affective, or psychomotor rigor of each expected outcome.

- *Enduring Understandings:* Enduring understandings are statements summarizing the important ideas and core processes that are central to a discipline and have lasting value beyond the classroom (National Coalition of Core Arts Standards, 2014).

- *Essential Questions:* Essential questions are questions that lie at the heart of a subject or a curriculum and promote inquiry and ultimately an emergence of a subject (National Coalition of Core Arts Standards, 2014).

- *Performance Standards:* Performance standards are the discipline-specific, grade-by-grade articulations/levels of student achievement (National Coalition of Core Arts Standards, 2014). Outside of the context of the National Core Arts Standards, performance standards are commonly referred to as instructional objectives (Wesolowski, 2015). The performance standards, similar to anchor standards, contain verbs embedded within educational taxonomies and provide additional information related to the specific cognitive rigor of each expected outcome. An important feature of performance standards is that they specify a certain level of performance to be classified into a specific category of achievement. In the 2014 standards, these are evidenced by the degrees of proficiency (e.g., novice, intermediate, proficient, accomplished, advanced).

- *Type of Scoring Device(s):* This type of instrument is used to collect evidence of student behaviors, including but not limited to checklists, rating scales, criteria-specific rating scales, rubrics, multiple-choice items, matching items, essays, matching tests.

- *Student Assessment Task(s):* Types of tasks are the specific behaviors expected of the student to perform on the test, including selected responses (e.g., multiple-choice items, true-and-false items, matching items), constructed responses (short-answer items, extended-response items) or performance tasks (e.g., checklist items, rating scale criteria, rubric criteria).

- *Item/Criteria Types:* Item-types describe the type of items used to capture the student behavior (e.g., multiple choice, fill-in-the-blank, short answer) and criteria types describe the evaluative criteria included in a checklist, rating scale, or rubric.

Assessment Blueprint Vignette

Mr. John Davidson is a middle school band director, and the focus of his instructional unit is rhythm identification and rhythm performance. There is a particular set of rhythms that Mr. Davidson is introducing to the students through the careful selection of ensemble repertoire. The rhythms include various combinations of eighth notes and quarter notes presented in common, 4/4 time. There are ten variations of rhythms in the music on which he would like his students to focus. The primary outcome (e.g., artistic process) is to have the students be able to *perform* the rhythms independently, accurately, and musically within the context of the musical pieces. In order to facilitate an instructional path toward this outcome, he identifies three specific educational objectives he would like to see realized by his students: (a) students will be able to identify the rhythms aurally when performed in the context of a music selection, (b) students will be able to perform the rhythms accurately in the context of a sight-reading exercise, and (c) students will be able to perform the rhythms independently, accurately, and musically in the context of the musical repertoire. These objectives fit into the considerations of two artistic process components from the 2014 Standards: (a) analyze and (b) present. More specifically, the objectives are aligned to two anchor standards: (a) analyze the structure and context of varied musical works and their implications for performance and (b) perform expressively, with appropriate interpretation and technical accuracy, and in a manner appropriate to the audience and context. The three distinct educational objectives described above call for three distinct assessments. Therefore, each of the three assessments is found in the assessment blueprint for this particular instructional unit (see Figure 4.6).

Across all three assessments and as indicated in the example assessment blueprint, the artistic process to be assessed in this unit is *performing* along with two artistic process components: (a) *analyze* and

(b) *present*. This instructional unit consists of two anchor standards collectively across the three assessments: (a) *analyze the structure and context of varied musical works and their implications for performance* and (b) *perform expressively, with appropriate interpretation and technical accuracy, and in a manner appropriate to the audience and context.*

The purpose of the first assessment is to evaluate students' abilities to *aurally and visually identify rhythmic structures found in the music repertoire*. It is an educator-created rhythm identification test that is selected-response in nature. Specifically, the test will be scored based upon students' responses to various multiple-choice, matching, short-answer, and fill-in-the-blank items.

The purpose of the second assessment is to evaluate students' abilities to *perform rhythmic structures found in the music repertoire in the context of a sight-reading test*. It is an educator-created sight-reading test that is a performance task. Specifically, the test will be scored based upon students' performances of the isolated rhythms and will be scored using the rhythm and pulse accuracy rubric from the MCA Novice Performance Evaluation.

The purpose of the third assessment is to evaluate students' abilities to *perform rhythmic structures found in the music repertoire in the context of the music literature*. It is a performance test of the musical repertoire and is considered a performance task. Specifically, the test will be scored based upon students' performances of the rhythms found in the musical repertoire and will be scored using the tone production, rhythm and pulse accuracy, pitch and intonation accuracy, and expressive qualities/stylistic interpretation rubrics from the MCA Novice Performance Evaluation.

Assessment 2 and Assessment 3 will use the pre-established MCAs to evaluate the quality of student performance achievement. Assessment 1, however, is an educator-created selected-response test. In the case of an educator-created test, a table of specifications can be a helpful tool to craft a quality test aligned to instructional objectives.

Developing a Table of Specifications

A **table of specifications** (see Table 4.1) is a two-dimensional matrix that describes the content, structure, and learning outcomes of a specific assessment instrument. Tables of specification are most prominently used for selected-response tasks and can be beneficial to the educator as a method for aligning objectives, instruction, and assessment. In particular, the table of specifications can be used to describe the types and percentages of items on a test at each level of the cognitive domain, thereby providing a clear picture of the levels of thinking exhibited by the students when taking the test. This, in turn, not only provides an in-depth overview of

Table 4.1 Table of specifications that classifies learning outcomes in relation to content dimension and cognitive process dimension

	Cognitive Process Dimension			
Content Dimension	Remembering	Understanding	Applying	Analyzing
Quarter notes	• *Define* a quarter note • *Identify* notes as quarter notes using visual, music examples	• *Classify* quarter notes through visual, music examples • *Label* quarter notes through visual, music examples	–	–
Eighth notes	• *Define* an eighth note • *Identify* notes as eighth notes using visual, music examples	• *Classify* eighth notes through visual, music examples • *Label* eighth notes through visual, music examples	–	–
Quarter note/eighth note combinations	• *Explain* the difference between quarter notes and eighth notes	–	• *Solve* missing note values in measures based upon remainder of available note values	• *Differentiate* between a quarter note pulse and eighth note pulse through aural, musical examples • *Identify* eighth note and quarter note patterns through aural, music examples • *Differentiate* quarter note patterns, eighth note patterns, and mixed quarter/eighth note patterns through aural, music examples • *Analyze* measures using the rhythm labeling method taught in class

student achievement at various cognitive levels but can also provide valuable information for how items perform across various cognitive levels when analyzing classroom assessment data (see Chapter 8).

A table of specifications is displayed as a two-dimensional matrix because it provides the visual relationship between the content knowledge on a test (the rows) and the cognitive processes for each content element (the columns). The content knowledge represents the learning outcomes for the instructional unit. Each of the learning outcomes contains measurable behaviors students should exhibit that are specifically associated with a certain cognitive level. The cognitive levels are the categories of cognitive difficulties (e.g., Bloom's six categories including knowledge, comprehension, application, analysis, synthesis, and evaluation).

Table of Specifications Vignette

The first assessment documented in the assessment blueprint is an educator-created, selected-response test and is therefore a good candidate to develop with the aid of a table of specifications. In order to develop a table of specifications, it is first important to review both the anchor standards and performance standards of the instructional unit and consider how the purpose of the test fits into the broad educational outcomes of the unit. In the case of this example, the anchor standard for the test is, "Analyze the structure and context of varied musical works and their implications for performance." The educator identifies the ensemble as a novice ensemble, and the performance standard under the artistic process reads as follows: *Demonstrate, using music-reading skills where appropriate, how knowledge of formal aspects of musical works inform prepared or improvised performances.* In particular with this test, the students are being asked to aurally and visually identify rhythmic structures found in the music repertoire. The educator has indicated that the word *identify* is a foundational consideration for what he is trying to assess.

Defining Learning Outcomes

Although the word *identify* is often found in the lower levels of many educational taxonomies, it in itself is too broad of a consideration for the specific skills and abilities underscoring the learning outcomes Mr. Davidson has set forth in his instructional unit. The next step for Mr. Davidson to consider is the specific content elements he would like to test the students on. He decides that he would like to test the students on the following three content elements:

1. Quarter notes
2. Eighth notes
3. Quarter note/eighth note combinations

He then considers his instructional unit and the specific instructional objectives embedded within the unit. In the context of the test he is developing, he considers how he wants the students to engage with each of the content elements based upon varying levels of cognitive thinking. To address this, he uses Bloom's Cognitive Taxonomy as a guide to define the specific learning outcomes of the instructional unit and related test. A few thoughts come to mind when he considers the six ordering levels and verbs associated with the taxonomy. In regard to the quarter notes element, he would like his students to demonstrate the following knowledge:
   By the end of the instructional unit:

1. Students will *define* a quarter note.
2. Students will *identify* notes as quarter notes using visual, music examples.
3. Students will *classify* quarter notes through visual, music examples.
4. Students will *label* quarter notes through visual, music examples.

In regard to the eighth notes element, he would like his students to demonstrate the following knowledge:
   By the end of the instructional unit:

5. Students will *define* an eighth note.
6. Students will *identify* notes as eighth notes using visual, music examples.
7. Students will *classify* eighth notes through visual, music examples.
8. Students will *label* eighth notes through visual, music examples.

In regard to the quarter note/eighth note combinations element, he would like his students to demonstrate the following knowledge:
   By the end of the instructional unit:

9. Students will *explain* the difference between quarter notes and eighth notes.
10. Students will *solve* missing note values in measures based upon remainder of available note values.
11. Students will *differentiate* between a quarter note pulse and eighth note pulse through aural, musical examples.

12. Students will *identify* eighth note and quarter note patterns through aural, music examples.
13. Students will *differentiate* quarter note patterns, eighth note patterns, and mixed quarter/eighth note patterns through aural, music examples.
14. Students will *analyze* measures using the rhythm labeling method taught in class.

Table 4.1 is a table of specifications that organizes each of the learning outcomes into a 2 x 2 matrix in order to visually demonstrate their relationship to their respective content and cognitive process dimensions.

Choosing Appropriate Item-Types

After considering the levels of cognitive knowledge he wants his students to demonstrate, Mr. Davidson considers the most appropriate item-type to best capture those particular behaviors. For the purpose of this assessment, he considers four types of possible items: multiple choice, matching, fill-in-the-blank, and short answer.

Multiple Choice

Multiple-choice items are the most versatile item-type for effectively and efficiently assessing learning outcomes at multiple cognitive levels. Multiple-choice items consist of three parts: (a) stem, (b) distractors, and (c) keyed alternative. The stem is the first part of the item that states either the problem or question to be solved. The distractors are the alternative choices that are incorrect. The keyed alterative is the correct answer to the question. Advantages to using multiple-choice items include the versatility in easily addressing the multiple cognitive domains and ability and to broadly represent instructional material, the ability for students to concretely think on the problem at hand (versus thinking about constructing answers), and providing diagnostic insight into students' thinking when they select a distractor. The disadvantages include the inability of a student to formulate their own ideas, ability of a student to easily guess, and the time it takes an educator to construct a high-quality item.

Matching

Matching items include two (or more) lists of adjacent words, symbols, images, or phrases. The purpose of a matching item is for the test taker to recognize, make an association, or classify various options within the two (or more) adjacent item lists. The advantage of using a matching item is that they are easy to construct and score, they are effective for evaluating knowledge of relationships, and they allow for the use of visual imagery that may be beneficial to younger students or students with certain preferences for visual learning. The disadvantages are that they do not foster higher-order thinking skills, they foster rote memorization and, as students match items, the items toward the end of the list lend themselves to being *giveaways*.

Fill-in-the-Blank and Short Answer

Fill-in-the-blank and short-answer items require a word, number, symbol, or short constructed response answer. The advantages of using this type of an item are its ease to construct, its versatility in assessing students at multiple cognitive levels, and the lower chance of a student guessing correctly. The disadvantages include the educator's sometimes needed subjectivity to the *correctness* of a response.

There are many other item-types, including checklists, true/false, essays, and transformation error correction. Nitko and Brookhart (2011) provide detailed information on item construction suggestions, advantages/disadvantages of various item-types, and considerations toward validity and reliability that may be beneficial to the music educator for developing high-quality items for cognitive tests.

Timing

The next task for Mr. Davidson to consider is the allotment of time he has for the students to take the test and how many items should be written for each learning target. There are some rules of thumb to follow when considering how long it takes for a student to answer a particular item-type. According to Notar et al. (2004):

- True/false: 15 seconds
- A seven-item matching exercise: 60–90 seconds
- A four-response option knowledge-level multiple choice: 30 seconds
- A four-response option application-level multiple choice: 60 seconds
- Any test item that asks students to solve, analyze, synthesize, or evaluate a problem: 30–60 seconds
- Short answer: 30–45 seconds
- Essay: 60 seconds for each point to be compared or contrasted
- Fill-in-the-blank: 30 seconds

Table 4.2 provides a schematic of the total number of items, the percentage of the test the learning target is tested, and the amount of time it is anticipated that each student will spend on each learning target.

Table 4.2 Table of specifications that outlines the dimensions, domains, items, and timing considerations for each learning outcome

Learning Outcomes (SWBAT . . .)*	Content Element	Domain	Item-type	No. of Items	% of Test	Time (m/s)
Define a quarter note	Quarter notes	Remembering	Short answer	1	1.4%	0:45
Define an eighth note	Eighth notes	Remembering	Short answer	1	1.4%	0:45
Identify notes as quarter notes using visual, music examples	Quarter notes	Remembering	Multiple choice	10	14.9%	5:00
Identify notes as eighth notes using visual, music examples	Eighth notes	Remembering	Multiple choice	10	14.9%	5:00
Explain the difference between quarter notes and eighth notes	Quarter note/ eighth note combinations	Remembering	Short answer	1	1.4%	0:45
Classify quarter notes through visual, music examples	Quarter notes	Understanding	Matching	2	2.9%	3:00
Label quarter notes through visual, music examples	Quarter notes	Understanding	Fill-in-the-blank	6	8.7%	3:00
Classify eighth notes through visual, music examples	Eighth notes	Understanding	Matching	2	2.9%	3:00
Label eighth notes through visual, music examples	Eighth notes	Understanding	Fill-in-the-blank	6	8.7%	3:00
Solve missing note values in measures based upon remainder of available note values	Quarter note/ eighth note combinations	Applying	Fill-in-the-blank	6	8.7%	3:00

Learning Outcomes (SWBAT . . .)*	Content Element	Domain	Item-type	No. of Items	% of Test	Time (m/s)
Differentiate between a quarter note pulse and eighth note pulse through aural, musical examples	Quarter note/ eighth note combinations	Analyzing	Multiple choice	6	8.7%	3:00
Identify eighth note and quarter note patterns through aural, music examples	Quarter note/ eighth note combinations	Analyzing	Multiple choice	6	8.7%	3:00
Differentiate quarter note patterns, eighth note patterns, and mixed quarter/eighth note patterns through aural, music examples	Quarter note/ eighth note combinations	Analyzing	Multiple choice	6	8.7%	3:00
Analyze measures using the rhythm labeling method taught in class	Quarter note/ eighth note combinations	Analyzing	Fill-in-the-blank	6	8.7%	3:00
Totals				**69**	**100%**	**39:15**

*Students will be able to . . .

Balancing Learning Outcomes, Cognitive Rigor, and Test Time

The test construction process can quickly become daunting when considering the multiple content elements; appropriateness of items; ability of items to validly, reliably, and fairly collect behavioral information; the amount of time it takes a student to engage with a particular item; the levels of rigor in relation to the learning outcomes; and the overall expectations of your students. The benefit of implementing a table of specifications for the test creation process is to have a visual tool to help consider all of these relationships.

Table 4.3 organizes the learning outcomes by cognitive domain. The result indicates that 34% (23 items, 12 minutes and 45 seconds) of the test is remembering items, 23.2% of the test (16 items, 12 minutes) is understanding items, 8.7% of the test (6 items, 3 minutes)

Table 4.3 Table of specifications sorted by cognitive domain

Learning Outcomes (SWBAT ...)*	Content Element	Domain	Item-type	No. of Items	% of Test	Time (m/s)
Define a quarter note	Quarter notes	Remembering	Short answer	1	1.4%	0:45
Define an eighth note	Eighth notes	Remembering	Short answer	1	1.4%	0:45
Identify notes as quarter notes using visual, music examples	Quarter notes	Remembering	Multiple choice	10	14.9%	5:00
Identify notes as eighth notes using visual, music examples	Eighth notes	Remembering	Multiple choice	10	14.9%	5:00
Explain the difference between quarter notes and eighth notes	Quarter note/ eighth note combinations	Remembering	Short answer	1	1.4%	0:45
Totals				23	34%	12:15
Classify quarter notes through visual, music examples	Quarter notes	Understanding	Matching	2	2.9%	3:00
Label quarter notes through visual, music examples	Quarter notes	Understanding	Fill-in-the-blank	6	8.7%	3:00
Classify eighth notes through visual, music examples	Eighth notes	Understanding	Matching	2	2.9%	3:00
Label eighth notes through visual, music examples	Eighth notes	Understanding	Fill-in-the-blank	6	8.7%	3:00
Totals				16	23.2%	12:00

Learning Outcomes (SWBAT . . .)*	Content Element	Domain	Item-type	No. of Items	% of Test	Time (m/s)
Solve missing note values in measures based upon remainder of available note values	Quarter note/ eighth note combinations	Applying	Fill-in-the-blank	6	8.7%	3:00
Totals				**6**	**8.7%**	**3:00**
Differentiate between a quarter note pulse and eighth note pulse through aural, musical examples	Quarter note/ eighth note combinations	Analyzing	Multiple choice	6	8.7%	3:00
Identify eighth note and quarter note patterns through aural, music examples	Quarter note/ eighth note combinations	Analyzing	Multiple choice	6	8.7%	3:00
Differentiate quarter note patterns, eighth note patterns, and mixed quarter/eighth note patterns through aural, music examples	Quarter note/ eighth note combinations	Analyzing	Multiple choice	6	8.7%	3:00
Analyze measures using the rhythm labeling method taught in class	Quarter note/ eighth note combinations	Analyzing	Fill-in-the-blank	6	8.7%	3:00
Totals				**30**	**43.5%**	**15:00**

*Students will be able to . . .

is applying items, and 43.5% of the items (30 items, 15 minutes) is analyzing items.

Table 4.4 organizes the learning outcomes by content elements. The result indicates that 27.9% (19 items, 11 minutes and 45 seconds) of the test is quarter note items, 27.9% of the test (19 items, 11 minutes and 45 seconds) is eighth note items, and 44.9% of the test (31 items, 15 minutes and 45 seconds) is quarter note/eighth note combination items.

Table 4.4 Table of specifications sorted by content element

Learning Outcomes (SWBAT . . .)*	Content Element	Domain	Item-type	No. of Items	% of Test	Time (m/s)
Define a quarter note	Quarter notes	Remembering	Short answer	1	1.4%	0:45
Identify notes as quarter notes using visual, music examples	Quarter notes	Remembering	Multiple choice	10	14.9%	5:00
Classify quarter notes through visual, music examples	Quarter notes	Understanding	Matching	2	2.9%	3:00
Label quarter notes through visual, music examples	Quarter notes	Understanding	Fill-in-the-blank	6	8.7%	3:00
Totals				**19**	**27.9%**	**11:45**
Define an eighth note	Eighth notes	Remembering	Short answer	1	1.4%	0:45
Identify notes as eighth notes using visual, music examples	Eighth notes	Remembering	Multiple choice	10	14.9%	5:00
Classify eighth notes through visual, music examples	Eighth notes	Understanding	Matching	2	2.9%	3:00
Label eighth notes through visual, music examples	Eighth notes	Understanding	Fill-in-the-blank	6	8.7%	3:00
Totals				**19**	**27.9%**	**11:45**

Learning Outcomes (SWBAT . . .)*	Content Element	Domain	Item-type	No. of Items	% of Test	Time (m/s)
Explain the difference between quarter notes and eighth notes	Quarter note/ eighth note combinations	Remembering	Short answer	1	1.4%	0:45
Solve missing note values in measures based upon remainder of available note values	Quarter note/ eighth note combinations	Applying	Fill-in-the-blank	6	8.7%	3:00
Differentiate between a quarter note pulse and eighth note pulse through aural, musical examples	Quarter note/ eighth note combinations	Analyzing	Multiple choice	6	8.7%	3:00
Identify eighth note and quarter note patterns through aural, music examples	Quarter note/ eighth note combinations	Analyzing	Multiple choice	6	8.7%	3:00
Differentiate quarter note patterns, eighth note patterns, and mixed quarter/eighth note patterns through aural, music examples	Quarter note/ eighth note combinations	Analyzing	Multiple choice	6	8.7%	3:00
Analyze measures using the rhythm labeling method taught in class	Quarter note/ eighth note combinations	Analyzing	Fill-in-the-blank	6	8.7%	3:00
Totals				31	44.9%	15:45

*Students will be able to . . .

Table 4.5 organizes the learning outcomes by item-type. The result indicates that 55.9% (38 items, 19 minutes) of the test is multiple-choice items, 5.8% of the test (4 items, 6 minutes) is matching items, 34.8% of the test (24 items, 12 minutes) are fill-in-the-blank items, and 4.2% of the test (3 items, 2 minutes and 15 seconds) is short-answer items.

Table 4.5 Table of specifications sorted by item-type

Learning Outcomes (SWBAT . . .)*	Content Element	Domain	Item-type	No. of Items	% of Test	Time (m/s)
Identify notes as quarter notes using visual, music examples	Quarter notes	Remembering	Multiple choice	10	14.9%	5:00
Identify notes as eighth notes using visual, music examples	Eighth notes	Remembering	Multiple choice	10	14.9%	5:00
Differentiate between a quarter note pulse and eighth note pulse through aural, musical examples	Quarter note/ eighth note combinations	Analyzing	Multiple choice	6	8.7%	3:00
Identify eighth note and quarter note patterns through aural, music examples	Quarter note/ eighth note combinations	Analyzing	Multiple choice	6	8.7%	3:00
Differentiate quarter note patterns, eighth note patterns, and mixed quarter/eighth note patterns through aural, music examples	Quarter note/ eighth note combinations	Analyzing	Multiple choice	6	8.7%	3:00
Totals				38	55.9%	19:00

Learning Outcomes (SWBAT . . .)*	Content Element	Domain	Item-type	No. of Items	% of Test	Time (m/s)
Classify quarter notes through visual, music examples	Quarter notes	Understanding	Matching	2	2.9%	3:00
Classify eighth notes through visual, music examples	Eighth notes	Understanding	Matching	2	2.9%	3:00
Totals				**4**	**5.8%**	**6:00**
Label quarter notes through visual, music examples	Quarter notes	Understanding	Fill-in-the-blank	6	8.7%	3:00
Label eighth notes through visual, music examples	Eighth notes	Understanding	Fill-in-the-blank	6	8.7%	3:00
Solve missing note values in measures based upon remainder of available note values	Quarter note/ eighth note combinations	Applying	Fill-in-the-blank	6	8.7%	3:00
Analyze measures using the rhythm labeling method taught in class	Quarter note/ eighth note combinations	Analyzing	Fill-in-the-blank	6	8.7%	3:00
Totals				**24**	**34.8%**	**12:00**
Define a quarter note	Quarter notes	Remembering	Short answer	1	1.4%	0:45
Define an eighth note	Eighth notes	Remembering	Short answer	1	1.4%	0:45
Explain the difference between quarter notes and eighth notes	Quarter note/ eighth note combinations	Remembering	Short answer	1	1.4%	0:45
Totals				**3**	**4.2%**	**2:15**

*Students will be able to . . .

Based on the resulting analysis, Mr. Davidson now has a clear picture of all the moving pieces of the test design process. He now has the ability to make informed changes to any of the items based upon the number of items representing various content elements, domains, item-types, number of items, percentages, or time considerations. Furthermore, he now can make informed decisions regarding the results of the testing procedure (see Chapter 8) after analyzing the test items.

Note that because Mr. Davidson is creating this test and using it for the first time, he specifically did not set a degree of mastery to accompany each of his instructional objectives. The first time a test is used, it is considered a *pilot test*. A pilot test is a "dress rehearsal" of the test operations that are implemented to determine whether problems with the test exist that need to be addressed (Lavrakas, 2008). In this case, once the test is given to the students and the data are collected, Mr. Davidson can explore item- and person-centered data (see Chapter 8) as well as any validity, reliability, and fairness considerations (see Chapter 5) that may impact the results of the test. After several iterations using the test with his students, Mr. Davidson will have a clear picture of the degrees of mastery students are expected to achieve as well as a better picture of how his instruction affects students' proficiency in relation to each of the learning objectives.

Summary

This chapter was designed to describe the process by which music educators develop student-learning outcomes, align assessment tasks with stated outcomes, and create scoring devices to collect data in order to provide timely, detailed, and meaningful feedback and analysis for both students and educators. A common method for examining student learning is through the application of educational taxonomies. Examples include Bloom's Taxonomy of Educational Objectives, Revised Bloom's Taxonomy, and the SOLO taxonomy. Educational taxonomies are often used to describe "levels" of learning taking place within the classroom and are a vital resource for crafting student-learning objectives. Employing a balance of multiple levels of thinking within an assessment plan is critical. Clearly articulating student-learning outcomes then creates transparency between the student and educator regarding what the student is expected to demonstrate upon completion of a lesson, unit, course, or program. Effective learning objectives are often described as having three major components: (a) conditions, (b) action verb (observable behavior), and (c) criteria. Conditions refer to the characteristics of the learners including but not limited to modeling, environment, context, and audience. The action verb (or observable behavior) refers to what knowledge, skill, or disposition the students will demonstrate for the teacher. Finally, criteria define the specific change in a specified behavior that is sought by the instructor. Educators are encouraged to preplan assessment processes prior to instruction in order to ensure valid, reliable, and fair inferences of student learning. There are several components in the preplanning process, including (a) an assessment blueprint, (b) a table of specifications, and (c) final considerations. An assessment blueprint is a concise plan of action that captures the multiple methods in which an educator intends to formally test students' academic performance in the classroom within a given instructional unit and serves as a method for preplanning how the educator will capture and evaluate the multiple streams of knowledge, skills, abilities, and/or dispositions students demonstrate aligned to expected learning outcomes. A table of specifications is a two-dimensional matrix that describes the content, structure, and learning outcomes of a specific assessment instrument and is predominantly used for selected response tasks as a beneficial means for aligning objectives, instruction, and assessment. Final considerations include item selection and construction, timing, and balancing outcomes, rigor, and test time. While the process of assessment can appear daunting, breaking the process down into specific steps to guide the learning of your students will ensure success within both your lessons and programs.

Activities and Worksheets

Class Activity 4.1: State Your Case!

Your administration has approached you about revising the local district curriculum. Among the topics under review is the learning taxonomy for the district moving forward. They have asked you to produce a white paper describing the strengths and weaknesses of each taxonomy and provide an expert opinion for which taxonomy best fits the learning of your music students, citing specific examples. Once this is complete, your professor will have you complete one (or more) of the following:

- Submit your findings in written form.
- Present your findings in a school board setting.
- Participate in a one-on-one interview similar to working with an administrator.

Class Activity 4.2: What Composes a Complete Musician?

In pairs, develop a list of activities that your students encounter within your program on a regular basis. This should include all activities that promote comprehensive musical development. Once lists are complete, trade lists with the group to your left and (a) review the list, (b) add any items you feel were omitted, (c) combine any that are similar, and (d) eliminate any that are redundant. Once these edits are complete, review your edits with your neighbors and compile these tasks into a master list.

Once the list is complete, separate these tasks into the following categories:

Knowledge (Cognitive)	Skill (Psychomotor)	Disposition (Affective)

Class Activity 4.3: Critical Thinking in the Music Classroom

Using the task list developed in *Class Activity 4.1*, have your group develop a list of action verbs that are necessary to successfully demonstrate complete musicianship. Once this list is compiled, organize the action verbs into the levels of thinking. Write a short rationale for inclusion of verbs in each category.

Knowledge	Understanding	Application	Analysis	Synthesis	Creation

Class Activity 4.4: Developing Your Objectives

Select one of the activities above about which you will compose a learning objective. Use the formula below (ABCs of learning) to create a specific learning outcome for your students.

Audience:		(For whom is this objective intended?)
Behavior:		(What are you asking your students to do? What action are you seeking to develop or improve?)
Conditions:		(What are the parameters? What is given? What is the time frame?)
Degree:		(What will be your indicators that learning has occurred? What are your expectations for learning?)

Write your complete objective here. Circle your action verb, underline your conditions, square your degree, and include your audience in parentheses at the end.

_____

_____

_____

_____

Class Activity 4.5: Developing an Assessment Blueprint

Using Figure 4.6 as a model, develop an assessment blueprint for a mock instruction unit. Include at least two assessments for the instructional unit: (a) a performance assessment and (b) a cognitive test. In the assessment blueprint, include the following considerations:

1. Class/student level
2. Instructional unit
3. Artistic process(es) to be assessed
4. Artistic processes component(s) to be assessed
5. Anchor standard(s) to be assessed
6. Performance standard(s) to be assessed

For each of the two individual assessments, provide the following:

1. Purpose of the assessment
2. Enduring understanding(s)
3. Essential question(s)
4. Performance standard(s)
5. Anchor standard(s)
6. Artistic processes component(s)
7. Artistic process(es)
8. Scoring device name
9. Type of scoring device
10. Student task(s)
11. Item/criteria type(s)

Class Activity 4.6: Developing a Table of Specifications

Using Table 4.1 as a model, develop a table of specifications for a mock cognitive test. In the table of specifications, include the following considerations:

1. Learning outcomes
2. Content elements
3. Domains

4. Item types
5. Number of items
6. Percentage of the test
7. Time considerations

Notes

1. Retrieved from www.nwlink.com/~donclark/hrd/Bloom/psychomotor_domain.html.
2. Ensure that behavior here is the learning actions of the students and should not be confused with behavior within the context of classroom management.
3. Understanding and performing are often used in long-term outcomes based on their inherent duality in functioning both as a noun and a verb (Wiggins & McTighe, 2005). Therefore, understanding and performing are more appropriate to include in program or course level (i.e., global objectives and/or educational objectives; Wesolowski, 2015).
4. Adapted from Doran (1981).

References

Anderson, L. W., & Krathwohl, D. R. (Eds.). (2001). *A taxonomy for learning, teaching, and assessing: A revision of Bloom's Taxonomy of Educational Objectives.* Boston, MA: Allyn & Bacon.
Ausubel, D. P., & Robinson, F. G. (1969). *School learning: An introduction to educational psychology.* New York, NY: Holt, Rinehart & Winston.
Biggs, J. B., & Collis, K. (1982). *Evaluating the quality of learning: The SOLO taxonomy.* New York: Academic Press.
Bloom, B. (Ed.). (1956). *Taxonomy of Educational Objectives, the classification of educational goals: Handbook I: Cognitive domain.* New York: McKay.
Dave, R. H. (1970). Psychomotor levels. In R. J. Armstrong (Ed.), *Developing and writing behavioral objectives.* Tucson, AZ: Educational Innovators Press.
Doran, G. T. (1981). There's a SMART way to write management's goals and objectives. *Management Review, 70,* 36.
Fink, L. D. (2003). *Creating significant learning experiences: An integrated approach to designing college courses.* San Francisco, CA: Jossey-Bass.
Gagné, R. M. (1965). *The condition of learning and theory of instruction.* New York, NY: Holt, Rinehart & Winston.
Gagné, R. M., & Briggs, L. J. (1974). *The principles of instructional design.* New York, NY: Holt, Rinehart & Winston.
Hook, P., & Mills, J. (2011). SOLO taxonomy versus Bloom's taxonomy. *HookED Wiki.* Retrieved from http://pamhook.com/wiki/SOLO_Taxonomy_versus_Bloom's_Taxonomy
Krathwohl, D. R., Bloom, B. S., & Masia, B. B. (1964). *Taxonomy of Educational Objectives: Handbook II: Affective domain.* New York, NY: David McKay Co.
Lavrakas, P. J. (2008). Pilot test. In *Encyclopedia of survey research methods.* Thousand Oaks, CA: Sage Publications. doi:10.4135/9781412963947
Mager, R. F. (1984). *Preparing instructional objectives* (2nd ed.). Belmont, CA: Lake Publishing.

Marzano, R. J., & Kendall, J. S. (2007). *The new Taxonomy of Educational Objectives*. Thousand Oaks, CA: Sage Publications.

Merriam-Webster Online Dictionary. (n.d.). *Taxonomy*. Retrieved from www.merriam-webster.com/dictionary/taxonomy

National Coalition of Core Arts Standards. (2014). *National Core Arts Standards: A conceptual framework for arts learning*. Retrieved from www.nationalartsstandards.org/sites/default/files/NCCAS%20%20Conceptual%20Framework_0.pdf

Nitko, A. J., & Brookhart, S. M. (2011). *Educational assessment of students*. Boston, MA: Pearson.

Notar, C. E., Zuelke, D. C., Wilson, J. D., & Yunker, B. D. (2004). The table of specifications: Insuring accountability in teacher made tests. *Journal of Instructional Psychology, 31*(2), 115–129.

O'Toole, P. (2003). *Shaping sound musicians*. Chicago, IL: GIA Publications.

Payne, P., Burrack, F., Parkes, K. A., & Wesolowski, B. (2019). An emerging process of assessment in music education. *Music Educators Journal, 105*(3), 36–44.

Webb, N. (1997). *Research monograph number 6: Criteria for alignment of expectations and assessments on mathematics and science education*. Washington, DC: CCSSO.

Wesolowski, B. C. (2015). Tracking student achievement in music performance: Developing student-learning objectives for growth model assessment. *Music Educators Journal, 102*, 39–47.

Wiggins, G. P., & McTighe, J. (2005). *Understanding by design*. Alexandria, VA: Association for Supervision and Curriculum Development.

5 Validity, Reliability, and Fairness in Classroom Tests

Brian C. Wesolowski

Chapter Overview

This chapter addresses the evaluation of music classroom testing quality using three key indicators: **validity**, **reliability**, and **fairness**.

Learning Expectations for the Chapter

- Define and describe a latent construct.
- Define and describe validity, reliability, and fairness in the context of large-scale testing.
- Define and describe validity, reliability, and fairness in the context of music classroom testing.
- Describe processes to evaluate the validity, reliability, and fairness of classroom testing outcomes.

Essential Questions for the Chapter

- What makes the testing of musical constructs so difficult?
- Why are validity, reliability, and fairness important considerations when making inferences about student achievement in the music classroom?
- How can we ensure that we truly capture student learning through the process of testing?

When we hear the word *test*, we may automatically consider a multiple-choice, fill-in-the-blank, or a true-and-false exam. We may think of the process of sitting down at a desk with a pencil and paper or sitting in front of a computer answering systematically crafted questions that reflect some type of content knowledge. As music students and music performers, the word test, in the context of music, specifically, might automatically bring about the idea of a performance or playing test, as the field does not usually engage in standardized tests or written classroom exams. According to Cizek (2012), however, a test can be more broadly conceptualized as "simply a data collection procedure; more precisely, . . . a sample of behavior(s) taken and interpreted under specified, systematic, and uniform conditions" (p. 3). As Cizek suggests, the concept of a test is frequently interpreted too narrowly, and it is often mistaken as referring to a specific format for data collection instead of the broad, structured process used to collect the information. Using Cizek's definition, a test, in the context of a music classroom, can be considered *any circumstance in which a teacher makes a systematic observation of students' musical behavior*. As music teachers, we test our students every day, whether the information is collected for diagnostic, formative, or summative reasons, formally or informally, in the context of a cognitive task or a performance task, through general, day-to-day observations or systematic, scheduled examinations. A test, broadly considered, is not necessarily the mechanism for how a music teacher evaluates students' musical behaviors or the particular method of scoring or grading, but the notion that some type of information about a student's knowledge, skills, abilities, or dispositions is being systematically collected.

The testing and **measurement** of any musical behavior is an abstract concept. If we were to measure the height of a person, we could use a physical ruler with inches as our unit of measurement. If we were to measure the weight of a person, we could use a physical scale with pounds as our unit of measurement. In both cases, the measurement is made with a pre-established physical instrument and is conducted with some unit of measurement that is specifically being used to make comparisons or more or less of the attribute being measured. Does one person have more or less height than another person? Does one person have more or less weight than another person? If we were to measure the performance achievement of a clarinetist, however, the process becomes much more complex. How would we define performance achievement? What musical behaviors would we evaluate about the clarinetist that reflect the idea of performance achievement? How would we collect evidence of performance achievement? What type of measurement instrument would we use to evaluate performance achievement? How would we score the student based upon the behaviors we observe? Unlike the physical sciences, where testing and measurement are concrete, physical, and utilize a specified unit of measurement, testing and measurement in the behavioral sciences, including music, are abstract, psychological, and do not often utilize a specified unit of measurement.

From a theoretical testing perspective, tests of musical behavior measure some type of unobservable, or *latent*, construct (Loevinger, 1957). Latent constructs (sometimes referred to as latent traits, behaviors, or attitudes) can be defined as "*any construct that cannot be directly measured but rather inferred through the measurement of secondary behaviors"* (Wesolowski, 2019). More specifically, a latent construct:

> is an idea developed or "constructed" as a work of informed, scientific imagination; that is, it is a theoretical idea developed to explain and organize some aspects of existing knowledge . . . the construct is much more than a label; it is a dimension understood or inferred from its network of interrelationships[.]
>
> (APA, AERA, & NCME, 1974, p. 29)

Musical constructs such as musical aptitude, music performance achievement, musical preference, ear-training ability, or any other music content knowledge or music performance expectation, for example, cannot be measured with physical instruments and there are no specified units of measurement associated with the constructs. In most of the educational, behavioral, and psychological sciences, such as music, these constructs cannot be directly measured; rather, they are *inferred* using secondary, observable behaviors that represent the latent construct. The test itself acts as an operational definition of the latent construct. The items (for a cognitive task) or criteria (for a performance task) included within a test are the secondary behaviors that are observable. The interactions between the items/criteria and the student are observable in the sense that the student engages with the items/criteria in order to demonstrate some level of achievement. If it is a cognitive task, the student directly engages with the item by responding to it. If it is a performance task, the student indirectly engages with the criteria (mediated by the teacher scoring the performance). **Inferences** are the conclusions that are made by the teacher about the adequacy of the test in regard to the latent construct being measured, the data-gathering procedures, the level of achievement of the student, and their interpretation of the data gathered from the test. Inferences are the link between the secondary, observable behaviors and the primary, unobservable construct (see Figure 5.1).

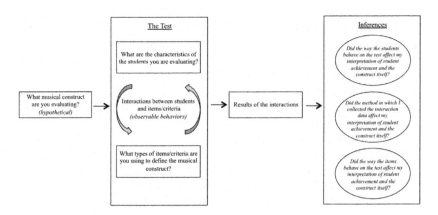

Figure 5.1 Making inferences from hypothetical constructs

As an example, the latent construct of music aptitude is an unobservable behavior that cannot be directly measured. As music teachers, we cannot simply hold a theoretical ruler up to a student and indicate that the student has certain amount of musical aptitude. Music aptitude, such as defined by Edwin Gordon's (1995) *Musical Aptitude Profile*, for example, is inferred based upon secondary, observable behaviors including students' interactions with test items associated with (a) tonal imagery (melody and harmony), (b) rhythm imagery (tempo and meter), and (c) musical sensitivity (phrasing, balance, and style). In Arnold Bentley's (1966) *Measures of Music Abilities*, music aptitude is inferred based upon secondary, observable behaviors including students' interactions with test items associated with (a) pitch discrimination, (b) tonal memory, (c) chord analysis, and (d) rhythmic memory. In these two examples, different measures developed by both Gordon and Bentley include different observable behaviors (i.e., domains and test items), but both purport to measure the same latent construct of musical aptitude.

As another example, music performance achievement is an unobservable behavior that cannot be directly measured. In the National Association for Music Education's (NAfME) (2018) *Concert Band Assessment Form*, music performance achievement is defined based upon secondary, observable behaviors including an ensemble's ability to perform a task associated with (a) sound quality (tone quality and pitch), (b) technical accuracy (technique and rhythm), (c) musicality (interpretation, musicianship, dynamics, and breath), and (d) stage deportment. In the Florida Bandmasters Association (FBA) (2018) *Concert Band Assessment Form*, music performance achievement is inferred based upon secondary, observable behaviors including an ensemble's ability to perform a task associated with (a) performance fundamentals (tone quality, intonation, balance, blend, sonority, and physical articulation), (b) technical preparation (note accuracy, rhythmic accuracy, precision, entrances, releases, interpretive articulation, clarity of articulation, technique, stability of pulse, dynamics observed, and transitions), and (c) musical effect (expression, shaping of line, style, interpretation, phrasing, tempo, and dynamic expression). In this example, different measures developed by both NAfME and FBA include different observable behaviors (i.e., domains and evaluative criteria), but both purport to measure the same latent construct of music performance achievement.

Learning Experience: Locate the performance assessment for large groups in your state. Then, locate the performance assessment for large groups in another state. Identify and list the observable behaviors in the assessment. Then, in groups, compare and contrast both state performance assessments and discuss the importance placed on each through the development of the given assessment.

In both the music aptitude and music performance achievement examples, the test developers each have a unique, but similar operational definition of the construct. So who is right, which measure is better, and what does this mean in the context of the music classroom? For a classroom music teacher, it is the teacher's responsibility to define the construct, outline the specific observable behaviors that define the construct, and ensure that instruction is aligned to the observable behaviors. For example, if a music teacher is collecting information about his or her students' rhythm identification achievement, rhythm identification achievement is the latent construct. Rhythm identification achievement, theoretically, is an unobservable construct in itself. It becomes the teacher's job to operationally define the latent construct through some type of test. Whether the data collection process is a cognitive task (e.g., multiple-choice items, dictation items) or a performance task (e.g., performance criteria via a rating scale, rubric), the items/criteria that the students directly or indirectly interact with are the observable behaviors that represent the teacher's operational definition of rhythm identification achievement. Each student interacts with each item or criterion, either directly providing answers for each question for a cognitive task or being judged by the teacher for a performance task, resulting in multiple observable behaviors that represent the construct of rhythm identification achievement. It is then the teacher's job to make inferences of the student achievement based upon the collection of behaviors made. The most important question to ask in the music aptitude example, the music performance achievement example, and the rhythm identification achievement example is, *How good are the inferences about the student's achievement based upon the data collected from the observations?* In order to answer questions pertaining to the quality of inferences made from a test, three important indicators should be considered: validity, reliability, and fairness.

Learning Experience: Choose a performance task of your choice that you might use in your classroom. Design criteria that identify observable behaviors and your expectations as they relate to those given behaviors.

Traditional Perspectives of Validity, Reliability, and Fairness

Traditional views of validity, reliability, and fairness are most often written about in the context of large-scale, high-stakes testing (See Wesolowski & Wind, 2019 for detailed overview). Examples of these large-scale tests may include SATs, GREs, or other state-based competency exams. The strict, operational definitions that stem from these writings, however, are not entirely relevant for the application in classroom settings. In order to evaluate the quality (i.e., validity, reliability, and fairness) of the inferences gleaned from large-scale tests, psychometricians typically apply measurement models and statistical analyses to the collected observations that provide both quantitative and qualitative evidence of quality, each distinctly related to validity, reliability, and fairness considerations. In these contexts, validity, reliability, and fairness investigations are test-centered, external to the classroom, standardized, and student achievement–based. Classroom tests, on the other hand, are student-centered, internal to the classroom, non-standardized, and student-learning-based.

Classroom teachers are not particularly focused on how a specific classroom test performs; rather, they are more concerned with the how multiple classroom tests, together, can holistically provide information about student achievement to help understand, develop, foster, and improve student learning. Results of classroom testing are much more embedded into the instructional environment and are used to guide and facilitate student learning through cyclical teaching and learning processes. In these contexts, validity, reliability, and fairness investigations should be student-centered, internal to the classroom, non-standardized, and student-learning-based (see Table 5.1). Therefore, principles of validity, reliability, and fairness in the context of classroom teaching and learning should include different applications and considerations compared to those typically described from a large-scale testing perspective.

Table 5.1 Differences between large-scale tests and classroom tests

	Large-Scale Tests	*Classroom Tests*
Reporting	Standardized	Non-standardized
Purpose	Measurement of learning (summative)	Measurement for learning (formative and summative)
Context	Linear	Cyclical
Relevance	Achievement-based	Learning-based
Process	Mastery	Developmental
Situatedness	Norm-referenced/criterion-referenced	Individual learning–based
Consequences	Often high-stakes/formal	Often low-stakes/informal
Data-type	Quantitative	Quantitative and qualitative
Construct Complexity	Unidimensional	Multidimensional

(Continued)

Table 5.1 (Continued)

	Large-Scale Tests	*Classroom Tests*
Responsibility of Validity	Test publisher, test user	Teacher, student
Content Representativeness	Standards-based	Curriculum-based
Decision-making	Policy-based, program-based	Instructional-based, curriculum-based
Changes	External (outside classroom)	Internal (inside classroom)
Objectivity	Evaluated by statistical error	Evaluated by systematic procedures
Consequences	Accountability	Improvement of student learning

In order to consider validity, reliability, and fairness in the context of classroom assessment, it is important to first conceptualize and understand validity, reliability, and fairness in the context of large-scale testing contexts. Using these definitions and applications as a foundation, we can then build upon them to make them more meaningful and relevant for classroom use.

Validity

Validity, according to the *Standards for Educational and Psychological Testing* (AERA, APA, & NCME, 2014), is defined as follows:

> Validity refers to the degree to which evidence and theory support the interpretations of the test scores for proposed uses of tests. Validity is, therefore, the most fundamental consideration in developing tests and evaluating tests. The process of validation involves accumulating relevant evidence to provide a sound scientific basis for the proposed score interpretations.
>
> (p. 11)

The validation process in large-scale assessment contexts includes gathering a combination of qualitative and quantitative evidence to support the inferences about student achievement in relation to the test itself. This evidence can include multiple types of validity, including three of the broadest validity types: criterion validity, content validity, and construct validity.

Criterion validity refers to the extent to which a test matches related outcomes of a similar test measuring the same construct (Cronbach & Gleser, 1965). From our earlier music aptitude example, we could test our students' music aptitude ability using Edwin Gordon's (1995) *Musical Aptitude Profile* and Arnold Bentley's (1966) *Measures of Music Abilities* and see how similarly the students perform on both measures. If there is a high correlation, meaning that the ordering of the students (from high-achieving to low-achieving) in terms of their test performance is similar, one could provide an argument for the criterion validity of the measures.

Content validity refers to how adequately the content of the test covers the construct being measured (Messick, 1989). From our earlier music performance achievement example, we would want to ensure that there is an adequate use of domains and items in a way that (a) satisfactorily describes and defines music performance achievement and (b) effectively separates students based upon varying music performance achievement levels. For example, if a music performance achievement measure altogether omits items related to intonation, an arguably important criterion for high-quality performance achievement, there is an argument for underrepresentation of the latent construct and a source of content invalidity. A result of this omission may also play a role in inadequately separating out students who satisfactorily perform their musical selections in tune from students who do not satisfactorily perform their musical selections in tune. Other considerations for content validity arguments include clarity in the writing and overall appropriateness for the items/criteria in relation to the construct.

Construct validity refers to how well the items function together to represent the construct being measured (Cronbach & Meehl, 1955). As Wesolowski (2018) notes:

> the development of criteria within the context of an assessment is, more broadly, the process of developing a hypothetical, latent construct. . . . Therefore, the development of assessments is dualistic: (a) to provide a means for measuring students, and (b) to develop a hypothetical latent construct . . . therefore, the [testing] results . . . not only provide information about student performance; more importantly, they provide diagnostic information about each of the latent constructs represented by the measurement instruments[.]
>
> (p. 151)

Because the latent construct being development is a hypothetical abstraction, evidence is needed for how well the items and/or criteria function together to define the construct. From our earlier music performance achievement example in the context of content validation, we would want to ensure that there is an adequate use of domains and items in a way that (a) satisfactorily describes and defines music performance achievement and (b) effectively separates students based upon varying music performance achievement levels. Construct validity is closely related to content validity in that the goals of the validation process are the same: to satisfactorily define the latent construct and to effectively separate students based upon their achievement. However, in the case of construct validity, the validation process becomes more concrete. We are interested in the difficulty range of the items/criteria (i.e., how easy the least difficult item is to how difficult the most difficult item is) in relation to the achievement range of the students (i.e., how low the least-achieving student is to how high the most-achieving is) as well as how the items and students interact throughout both ranges.

Most broadly, validity answers the question, *How strong of an argument can be made that the inferences drawn from the testing scores are truly representative of the student taking the test?* It is worth noting that tests themselves are not validated. It is the inferences, or meaning one derives from testing outcomes, that are validated.

Learning Experience: As an in-class discussion, describe a testing moment in your life that may have been invalid. Why did you feel this way? How would you describe the infringement upon validity? Discuss with your class.

Reliability

According to the *Standards for Educational and Psychological Testing* (AERA et al., 2014), reliability is defined as:

> the consistency over replications of the testing procedure. Reliability/ precision is high if the testing scores for each person are consistent over replications of the testing procedure and is low if the testing scores are not consistent over replications.

Evidence of reliability is demonstrated through various types of statistical estimations, including stability reliability coefficients (*Will the ordering of the students from high-scoring to low-scoring be the same across tests if repeated?*), equivalence coefficients (*How strong of a relationship is there between student scores using two or more tests of the same difficulty?*), internal consistency coefficients (*How consistent are the students' scores across the items within the same test?*), and rater reliability coefficients for performance tasks (*How consistent are raters with themselves and/ or with each other?*), for example. Reliability answers the question, *How stable are the measures?*

Fairness

Fairness, according to the *Standards for Educational and Psychological Testing* (AERA et al., 2014), is defined as the *responsiveness to individual characteristics and testing contexts so that testing scores will yield valid interpretations for intended uses.* Investigations into fairness often include considerations that may adversely affect student outcome scores, including but not limited to (a) test content (e.g., item content that may systematically favor or disadvantage some groups of students over others based on prior knowledge, experiences, level of interest or motivation, or other variables), (b) test context (e.g., aspects of the testing environment that systematically affect student outcome scores, such as clarity used in the test instructions, the complexity of vocabulary within the test items or tasks, or the language in which the test is administered), (c) test response (e.g., writing or speaking tasks may result in differences in responses that are unrelated to the construct due to cultural views related to wordiness or rate of speech, and survey items may result in differences in responses due to perceptions of social desirability), or (d) opportunity-to-learn (e.g., the extent to which individuals have had exposure to instruction or knowledge that affords them the opportunity to learn the content and skills targeted by the test). Fairness is the investigation of biases (i.e., systematic lower or higher scoring outcomes) against subgroups of students related to four considerations described above, including socioeconomic status, parental involvement, access to technology, gender, race, and parent's educational background, for example. Fairness answers the question, "Do all students receive equitable treatment during the testing process?"

Music Classroom Perspectives on Validity, Reliability, and Fairness

In the case of large-scale assessment, the three quality indicators of validity, reliability, and fairness are largely connected to the measurement of student achievement based upon scoring outcomes of standardized tests, external to the classroom. In order to provide grounded arguments for each of these indicators, an inference must be made about student achievement using a specified measurement model stemming from some theory of measurement. These theories can include Classical Test Theory, Generalizabilty Theory, or Item Response Theory (IRT), for example. From a large-scale testing perspective, measurement of student achievement for any educational, psychological, or behavioral construct, including music, can only be achieved via a measurement model. In making inferences about student achievement from their engagement with a large-scale test, the implementation of measurement models provides objective, empirical evidence that supports validity, reliability, and fairness arguments.

Applications of measurement models are inaccessible or even inappropriate for classroom music teachers. The statistical indices and other qualitative considerations that support item and construct analyses are not necessarily of day-to-day interest to the music teacher, and the time, energy, and effort to conduct such analyses would draw the teacher away from instructional time. Therefore, from a traditional validity perspective, there are no data to support a validity argument. Because replication is essential to reliability arguments, the student would need to be either judged by multiple people, the student would need to respond more than once to a prompt in order to evaluate the reliability of the assessment, or statistical reliability analyses would need to be conducted by the teacher to investigate the reliability of a test. Therefore, from a traditional reliability perspective, there are no data to support a reliability argument. The small number of students in any classroom, the embedded nature of the performance assessment, and the lack of statistical tools to support the analysis of bias makes fairness testing virtually impossible for the classroom music teacher. Therefore, from a traditional fairness perspective, there are no data to support a fairness argument. Although this is an oversimplification of validity, reliability, and fairness procedures, it is clear that there is an incompatibility of paradigms in considering the quality of the assessment contexts themselves or, more importantly, quality of the inferences gleaned from the assessment contexts (see Table 5.2).

Seeing this inconsistency, Brookhart (2003) called for the development of improved methodologies for evaluating the qualities of classroom

Table 5.2 Validity, reliability, and fairness in the context of large-scale assessments and classroom assessments

		Large-Scale Assessment	*Classroom Assessment*
Validity	*Purpose*	Purpose is meaningful inference of student achievement.	Purpose is meaningful inference of student learning.
	Measurement	Objective measurement of the student using a measurement model.	Implied measurement of the student using raw scores and qualitative interactions.
	Alignment	Knowledge/skill/ability/ disposition content is set forth by content standards.	Knowledge/skill/ ability/disposition content is set forth by learning objectives and instructional activities.
	Performance standards	Level of achievement is specified by performance standards using norm-referenced reporting (student classification) or criterion-referenced reporting (students on a continuum).	Level of achievement is specified by illustrative exemplars of student work at multiple achievement levels.
	Testing	Formal test is conducted externally and validity argument is made by test constructor and test user.	Formal and informal tests conducted internally and validity argument is made by teacher and student.
	Evidence for arguments	Statistical evidence supports validity argument.	Instructional decisions support validity argument.
Reliability	*Purpose*	Purpose is statistical evidence of stability of scores across multiple testing occasions.	Purpose is to attain sufficient information that demonstrates learning across instructional cycle.
	Interpretation	Statistical property of the score itself.	Qualitative property of teacher's diagnosis of student learning.
	Evidence	Small standard errors, high internal consistency.	Systematic classroom procedures aligned with test content.

(Continued)

Table 5.2 (Continued)

		Large-Scale Assessment	Classroom Assessment
Fairness	*Purpose*	Purpose is statistical evidence of construct-irrelevant variability stemming from non-assessment characteristics.	Purpose is to assure demonstration of learning is not limited by non-classroom characteristics.
	Test response	Statistical evidence of construct-irrelevant variability stemming from student characteristics.	Teacher provides varied and differentiated opportunities for students to demonstrate learning.
	Test content	Statistical evidence of construct-irrelevant variability stemming from test content.	Teacher demonstrates that the test content is aligned with learning objectives (appropriateness).
	Test context	Statistical evidence of construct-irrelevant variability stemming from testing context.	Students clearly understand what is being assessed and how to engage with the test.
	Test construct	Statistical evidence of construct-irrelevant variability stemming from response type.	Teacher uses varied types of assessments, such as cognitive tests, performance evaluations, portfolios, self-reflections.
	Opportunity-to-learn	Statistical evidence of construct-irrelevant variability stemming from opportunity-to-learn factors.	Teacher assures demonstration of learning is not affected by individual student characteristics.

assessments across all educational contexts through her notion of class-roometrics. Classroometrics, according to Brookhart,

> should take into account that classroom assessments provide infor-mation about students that immediately becomes part of their learn-ing environment and their own psychology . . . . the main actions of interest are relatively immediate, internal changes in the students who are measured.

(pp. 8–9)

Drawing on Brookhart's suggestions for improved quality control of class-room testing, Wesolowski (in press) provided suggestions for validity,

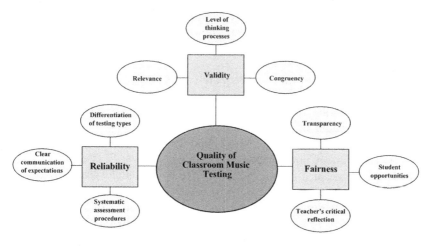

Figure 5.2 Considerations toward the quality of classroom music testing

reliability, and fairness considerations in classroom music testing that are more accessible, applicable, manageable, and relevant for music teaching and learning in the classroom. These considerations are more qualitative in nature and are based upon important questions to ask while crafting, implementing, and reflecting upon any classroom music testing circumstances. Figure 5.2 is an overview of these considerations.

Validity

In the context of classroom testing, validity can be defined as the confidence that a teacher has in the quality of the inferences they make about student-learning outcomes. There are three important considerations toward the validity of classrooms tests: (a) relevance, (b) levels of thinking processes, and (c) congruency.

Relevance

Relevance refers to the alignment between the content of the test and any related national/state standards and learning objectives that underscore the related teaching. There are three important questions to consider when evaluating validity with respect to relevance:

1. Is the content of the test properly aligned with the learning outcomes of the curricular unit?
2. Is the content of the test properly aligned with the content taught throughout the curricular unit?
3. Is the content of the test properly aligned with district, state, or national standards?

Level of thinking processes refers to the considerations of the cognitive rigor of the test in relation to the cognitive rigor of the course content and student abilities. There are four important questions to consider when evaluating validity with respect to level of thinking processes:

1. Is the difficulty of the test adequately matched to the student's ability level?
2. Is the difficulty of the test adequately matched to the instructional content taught in the classroom?
3. Does the difficulty of the test adequately match the ability represented by the student during class instruction?
4. Is the range of difficulty within the test adequately distributed?

Congruency refers to the relationship of the outcome of the test with previous patterns of student achievement. There are three important questions to consider when evaluating validity with respect to congruency:

1. Does the student's outcome of the test generally match the teacher's expected outcome?
2. Are there large groups of students who are unexpectedly overachieving or underachieving on the test?
3. Is the student bringing with him or her any prior experiences or unrelated knowledge that can affect the outcome of the test?

Reliability

In the context of classroom testing, **reliability** can be defined as the dependability of the test to adequately support the inferences made about the student learning outcomes. There are three important considerations toward the reliability of classroom tests: (a) differentiation of assessment types, (b) clear communication of expectations, and (c) systematic assessment procedures.

Differentiation of assessment types refers to the use of multiple assessment types to ensure a student's opportunity to demonstrate student-learning outcomes. There are four important questions to consider when evaluating reliability with respect to differentiation of assessment types:

1. Is there enough information to make an accurate judgment about the student's knowledge, skills, abilities, or dispositions being assessed?
2. If the student were to be tested again, is there confidence that he or she would be evaluated or respond to the questions in the same way?
3. What different types of information is the test soliciting in order to make a judgment of what the student knows or is able to do?
4. Are there other types of tests that can be used to elicit the knowledge, skills, abilities, or dispositions being tested?

Clear **communication of expectations** refers to the teacher ensuring that student has a comprehensive understanding of the teacher's learning outcome expectations. There are two important questions to consider when evaluating reliability with respect to communication of expectations:

1. Do the items (for cognitive tasks) or criteria (for performance tasks) clearly represent the learning outcomes and clearly communicate the expectations of the assessment?
2. Is there a set of illustrative student work that serves as exemplars for expectations across all achievement levels?

Systematic assessment procedures refer to the teacher ensuring student understanding, familiarity, and engagement with assessment procedures. There are four important questions to consider when evaluating reliability with respect to systematic assessment procedures:

1. Is the student comfortable with the testing process?
2. Is the testing procedure itself affecting the ability of the student to demonstrate the knowledge, skills, abilities, and/or dispositions being tested?
3. If a formal testing procedure is used, is the student aware of it and prepared for it?
4. Does the student understand how to engage with the test?

Fairness

In the context of classroom testing, fairness can be defined as the opportunities for a student to best demonstrate student-learning outcomes. There are three important considerations toward the fairness of classroom tests: (a) transparency, (b) student opportunities, and (c) teachers' critical reflection.

Transparency refers to the clear communication between teacher and student in regard to the testing context, testing content, and testing use. There are three important questions to consider when evaluating fairness with respect to fairness:

1. Does the student know what the test is going to be used for?
2. Is the student aware of any positive and/or possible negative consequences of the test?
3. Are the consequences of the testing procedure itself affecting the ability of the student to optimally demonstrate the knowledge, skills, abilities, and/or dispositions being tested?

Student opportunities refers to the ability of the student to adequately and accurately demonstrate their ability to meet student-learning outcomes in varied ways. There are five important questions to consider when evaluating fairness with respect to student opportunities:

1. Are students being provided multiple and varied opportunities to demonstrate what they know and what they are able to do?
2. Are accommodations necessary to allow for some students to best demonstrate their knowledge, skills, abilities, and/or dispositions being tested?
3. Are unnecessary accommodations being made for the student?
4. Is the student actively engaged day-to-day in the learning process and manner in which the learning process is being assessed?
5. Does the test authentically evaluate the day-to-day knowledge, skills, abilities, dispositions, and ways of being engaged with what is being tested?

Teachers' critical reflection refers to the teacher's considerations toward personal biases or stereotyping that may impede the testing process. There are five important questions to consider when evaluating fairness with respect to teachers' critical reflections:

1. Are assumptions of prior knowledge being made about the student that can affect the outcome of the test?
2. Is there flexibility between teacher expectations of the level of knowledge, skills, abilities, and/or dispositions being tested and the actual level of knowledge, skills, abilities, and/or dispositions being tested?
3. Are any teacher's stereotypes of the student affecting the testing process?
4. Are any group affiliations of the student, such as gender, ethnicity, ability level, instrument, affecting the testing outcome?
5. Are any personal interactions between the teacher and the student affecting the testing outcome?

Learning Experience: Select either a music or non-music course that you are currently enrolled in. Consider an individual testing context, specifically, and all of the testing contexts, broadly, that demonstrate your learning of the course content. What evidence of validity, reliability, and fairness have you witnessed? What is your evidence? Prepare a short presentation to share your findings with the class.

Summary

Musical constructs are difficult to measure because they are hypothetical in nature. More specifically, they are based upon secondary, observable behaviors that are used to infer the abstraction of the construct. As such, validity, reliability, and fairness considerations are necessary in order to ensure the quality of the inferences a teacher makes from testing outcomes. In the context of classroom testing, validity is defined as *the confidence that a teacher has in the quality of the inferences they make about student-learning outcomes* and is underscored by three important considerations: (a) relevance, (b) level of thinking processes, and (c) congruency. In the context of classroom testing, reliability is defined as *the dependability of the test to adequately support the inferences made about the student-learning outcomes* and is underscored by three important considerations: (a) differentiation of assessment types, (b) clear communication of expectations, and (c) systematic assessment procedures. In the context of classroom testing, fairness is defined as *the opportunities for a student to best demonstrate student-learning outcomes* and is underscored by three important considerations: (a) transparency, (b) student opportunities, and (c) teachers' critical reflection.

Activities and Worksheets

1. Reflect upon an instance when you were assessed in a music classroom setting in the context of a cognitive test and a performance test. Answer the following. Upon completion, discuss with the class.

Cognitive Test
What latent construct did this test measure?
What were the testing conditions?
Were the inferences the teacher concluded about your achievement of high quality? (yes or no)

Were the inferences the teacher concluded about your achievement valid? Explain.

Were the inferences the teacher concluded about your achievement reliable? Explain.

Were the inferences the teacher concluded about your achievement fair? Explain.

Performance Test

What latent construct did this test measure?

What were the testing conditions?

Were the inferences the teacher concluded about your achievement of high quality? (yes or no)

Were the inferences the teacher concluded about your achievement valid? Explain.

Were the inferences the teacher concluded about your achievement reliable? Explain.

Were the inferences the teacher concluded about your achievement fair? Explain.

---

2. Pair up with a classmate and construct a hypothetical scenario in which you are going to evaluate a student's achievement on a musical (a) cognitive task and (b) performance task. In both instances, describe any safeguards you would put in place to ensure the quality of the inferences you would make with regard to (a) validity, (b) reliability, and (c) fairness.

References

American Educational Research Association (AERA), American Psychological Association (APA), & National Council on Measurement in Education (NCME). (2014). *Standards for educational and psychological testing.* Washington, DC: American Educational Research Association.

American Psychological Association (APA), American Educational Research Association (AERA), & National Council on Measurement in Education (NCME). (1974). *Standards for educational and psychological tests and manuals.* Washington, DC: American Psychological Association.

Bentley, A. (1966). *Musical ability in children and its measurement.* New York: House Inc.

Brookhart, S. M. (2003, Winter). Developing measurement theory for classroom assessment purposes and uses. *Educational Measurement: Issues and Practice,* 5–12.

Cizek, G. J. (2012). An introduction to contemporary standard setting. In G. J. Cizek (Ed.), *Setting performance standards: Foundations, methods, and innovations* (2nd ed., pp. 3–14). New York, NY: Routledge.

Cronbach, L. J., & Gleser, G. C. (1965). *Psychological tests and personnel decisions.* Urbana: University of Illinois Press.

Cronbach, L. J., & Meehl, P. E. (1955). Construct validity in psychological tests. *Psychological Bulletin, 52,* 281–302.

Florida Bandmasters Association. (2018). *Florida Bandmasters Association adjudicator's comment sheet: Concert band.* Retrieved January 3, 2019, from http:// fba.flmusiced.org/media/1483/judgesheet-concertmus-with-rubric-rev2013-bullets.pdf

Gordon, E. E. (1995). *Musical aptitude profile (Grades 5–12).* Chicago, IL: GIA Publishers.

Loevinger, J. (1957). Objective tests as instruments of psychological theory. *Psychological Reports, 3,* 635–694.

Messick, S. (1989). Validity. In R. L. Linn (Ed.), *Educational measurement* (pp. 13–103). Washington, DC: American Council on Education and National Council on Measurement in Education.

National Association for Music Education. *National music adjudication coalition concert band or orchestra music assessment form.* Retrieved January 3, 2019 from https://nafme.org/wp-content/files/2016/04/Ensemble-Adjudication-Form-PDF.pdf

Wesolowski, B. C. (2018). Examination of the psychometric properties of the Model Cornerstone Assessments. In F. Burrack & K. A. Parkes (Eds.), *Applying Model Cornerstone Assessments in K-12 music: A research-supported approach* (pp. 151–180). Lanham, MD: Roman and Littlefield.

Wesolowski, B. C. (2019). Item response theory and music testing. In T. S. Brophy (Ed.), *The Oxford handbook of assessment, policy, and practice in music education* (pp. 479–503). New York: Oxford University Press.

Wesolowski, B. C. (in press). "Classroometrics": The validity, reliability, and fairness of classroom music assessments. *Music Educators Journal.*

Wesolowski, B. C., & Wind, S. A. (2019). Validity, reliability, and fairness in music testing. In T. S. Brophy (Ed.), *The Oxford handbook of assessment, policy, and practice in music education* (pp. 437–460). New York: Oxford University Press.

6 Performance Assessments

Kelly A. Parkes

Chapter Overview

This chapter illustrates the nature of performance assessments. The differences among performance assessments, authentic assessments, and alternative assessments are briefly explored. Processes for creating performance assessments are given and scoring devices are explained. The use of performance assessments is described and formative and summative uses are defined, with a final review of portfolio assessment.

Learning Expectations for the Chapter

- Define performance assessments.
- Contrast the uses of performance assessments.
- Construct scoring guides/devices for performance assessments.
- Identify scoring guides/devices already created.
- Recognize portfolio assessment.

Essential Questions for the Chapter

- What are the characteristics of performance assessments?
- What are the formative and summative uses?
- How are performance processes and performance products different?
- What are performance assessments?
- What are the advantages and disadvantages of portfolio assessment?

Introduction

Direct assessment is not a term typically used in music education. Direct assessment, in the wider assessment literature, was used by Lindvall (1961) to distinguish between direct and indirect assessment of educational outcomes. Indirect assessments or measures try to get information about one educational outcome by measuring something else, while direct assessments directly assess outcomes. An example of an indirect assessment or measure would be students' perceptions or thoughts *about* their learning (knowledge and skills), whereas a direct assessment measures an *observable demonstration* of learning. Direct assessments can be tests, quizzes, demonstrations, and reports, whereas indirect assessments typically illustrate students' perceptions about their learning or their opinions and thoughts about their knowledge and skills. Indirect measures are not as robust as direct measures because they may or may not represent reality. A student may report that they have a strong grasp on a musical concept; however, their teacher would not know unless they measured the students' knowledge directly. For more information about indirect assessments, please see Chapter 7.

Direct assessments allow teachers to expose what students know and can do, but they are not limited only to tests, quizzes, and worksheets. Direct assessments measure a defined educational outcome (for defining outcomes, please review Chapter 4) and identify the extent to which students demonstrate knowledge or skills. Direct assessments are those that are used within modern assessment approaches and encompass a variety of assessment formats. Other types of direct assessment are authentic assessment, alternative assessment, and performance assessment.

Authentic assessment is a type of direct assessment that measures the educational outcome both directly and authentically. Authentic assessments should not be confused with alternative assessments (Nitko, 1996). In the past, alternative assessments have been characterized as anything being "in opposition to standardized achievement tests and to multiple-choice . . . item formats" (Nitko, p. 243). Authentic assessments usually ask students to complete a task that is authentic to a context. That means that it has some sense of application, that it is direct, that it is based in reality, and that it encourages more open-ended thinking rather than focusing on one correct answer (Nitko, 1996). Early authentic assessment required students to synthesize and apply knowledge and skills using tasks that were replicated from authentic real-world situations. Context then becomes very important to consider. For example, individually performing in a playing test in the confines of a director's office is not authentic to the ways students demonstrate musical capabilities when performing with others in an ensemble. An authentic assessment should reflect the reality of a student's experience and applied expectation as closely as possible. Furthermore, the authenticity for the student should match the real-life experience as closely as possible. The preferred term in assessment terms is **performance assessment** due to its neutral position; however, this can be misleading in music education as the word *performance* is understood to be delivering a musical product rather than the broader meaning associated with authentic assessment.

Performance assessments or performance-based assessment tasks require that students apply their knowledge, usually from several areas, to demonstrate they can *perform* the learning target or goal. Performance assessments are considered to be authentic, realistic assessments because they are based in real-world expectations and are applied demonstrations of learning expectations. For example, the road test required for a driver's license is considered a performance assessment. Performance assessments can be seen as *alternative* assessments because they are an alternative to standardized multiple-choice tests. Performance assessment can be confusing in music because performing is what musicians do. It is easy to assume that all performances (e.g., the holiday concert or the state solo/ensemble competition) are performance assessments, but not all performances are assessed. Performance assessments also include making new music (composing, creating, or improvising a musical work) or producing a report that illustrates the learning goal (such as an analysis of a piece of music). These assessments address what students know *and* can do. Demonstrating a skill to teachers or classmates is an example of a performance assessment or a performance-based assessment task.

There are two parts to performance assessments: (a) the performance task itself and (b) a clearly defined scoring scheme or rubric, and both of these need to work together to complete an assessment of student learning. Typically, performance or authentic assessments entail that students *do* something that applies their knowledge and skills. In developing the assessment task, the teacher must make sure that what is asked of the student is indeed the actual performance defined by the learning outcome specifications. For example, the learning outcome of "know G major" is not specific enough as an assessment task because it does not define the means through which students are to demonstrate knowing. If, however, the learning outcome is "perform a G major scale," then a playing test requiring students to play a G major scale is the demonstration assessment task and the demonstration of the outcome. The next step (part 2) is to evaluate the quality of the demonstration of G major; that is, how well is the G major scale to be played? There are multiple criteria that might be considered in a musical demonstration, e.g., (a) the notes, (b) the rhythm, (c) the articulation, and (d) overall tone (as characteristic of the instrument being played). These criteria could be presented in a variety of ways, such as with a scoring device or rubric. Student demonstrations of learning, such as performances, are well suited to rubric assessments. Rubrics are also useful for assessing musical processes such as composing or analyzing a piece of music. It is important that teachers identify the explicit criteria that define the outcome for the assessment task. These criteria, when used by students, will guide them toward successful achievement of the learning outcome.

It is important to create scoring devices that measure criteria defined by the intended outcome and take into consideration the characteristics of the students. This means that the expectations for a beginner band student would be different to the expectations for a high school student. Therefore, the table of specifications created for a beginner band student would be different to a table of specifications created for a high school senior. Brophy (2003) illustrates a five-step process that allows us to develop our own assessments. Firstly, we need to consider the skill we are trying to assess. This should come from outcomes, written as "*students will be able to . . .*" and while some teachers choose these from the 2014 National Standards, or their respective state music standards, the choice of what specific knowledge or skill will be concentrated on is the teacher's. The teacher's expectations and the environment in which their music program operates are also important, alongside their learner's needs. The second step is to determine the appropriate assessment response mode (Brophy, 2003). When performing, students are actively making music. When creating music, students are generating new music, as composer, improviser, or arranger. When students are responding to music, they are using critical thinking skills that be seen in how they perceive, analyze, or interpret music. As teachers are measuring student skills and knowledge in these areas through performance assessments, it is essential to be clear about (a) what students need to do to demonstrate the outcome, (b) what role they need to undertake to demonstrate the outcome (perform, create, respond), and (c) what is the most authentic response mode to use in the assessment (Brophy, 2003). These must be reflective of the program expectations and become more authentic to students' learning when aligned with their interests. Assessments should be also relevant to the ways in which they students will use music in their lives. Thirdly, teachers should select the most appropriate assessment materials that will allow students to demonstrate what they can do or what they know (Brophy, 2003). This means using music examples that are developmentally appropriate or supplying staff paper or notation software. Fourth, assessment tasks need to be developed to have a specific set of procedures for students to demonstrate what they can do or what they know in ways that are relevant to them. These procedures need to very clear for students to understand. Finally, scoring devices must be developed, for example, rubrics or checklists or rating scales that contain the criteria (directly related to the outcomes set in step 1) and also have the levels of achievement. For example, in the MCAs, the levels defined are Emerging, Approaching Standard, Meeting Standard, and Exceeding Standard. This is because these scoring rubrics are tied directly to, and reflect the performance indicators, in the 2014 Standards.

Developing Criteria for Performance Assessments

It is important to recognize that there could be multiple sets of criteria that illustrate the characteristics of a musical performance, or composition, or analysis. Teachers should not confine criteria to a single set of indicators. Teachers must identify criteria that are important for, and responsive to, the current level of understanding and relevance in their own students. While it is easy to create a long list of criteria that characterize the learning that music students are to demonstrate, it is more important to consider the specific expectation for the performance task. When a list of criteria is long and extensive, students may not be able to focus on the expected learning and the teacher may find it difficult to differentiate achievement on each criterion while assessing the student's work. It is more efficient to measure meaningfully and more often than to have a scoring guide that is overly complicated and to use it only once. It is also more effective to measure the criteria specific to the learning developed through a task. The overall assessment process is more reliable using a scoring guide that is focused to the learning intent. It is also very important to review, revise, and refine performance task criteria and scoring devices over time as content and learning development changes. After using a scoring device with students, it is often the case that the teacher will make adjustments, which in turn will improve the usefulness of the device. Developing criteria that are observable is of paramount importance. Russell and Airasian (2008) suggest that teachers observe the following guidelines:

1. Select the performance or product of learning to be assessed and either complete the task yourself or imagine yourself performing it.
2. List the important aspects of the performance or product.
3. Try to limit the number of performance criteria so that all can be observed during the student performance.
4. If possible, discuss with peer teachers the important criteria demonstrated in the task.
5. Express the performance criteria in terms of observable student behaviors or product characteristics. Do not use ambiguous words that cloud the meaning of the performance criteria.
6. Arrange the performance criteria in the order in which they are likely to be observed.
7. Check for existing performance criteria before defining your own.
   (Russell & Airasian, 2008, pp. 214–215).

Learning Experience: Using an outcome (Common Anchor) from the 2014 National Standards, create a table with the following sections for a performance assessment.

1. The skill to be assessed (performing music, creating music, or recognizing musical sounds)
2. The appropriate response mode: the means through which students will demonstrate learning (e.g., performing, composing, or aurally identifying intervals)
3. The assessment materials (music scores, notation paper/software, or musical examples)
4. The assessment task (music performance, creating music, verbal responses)
5. The scoring guide (which specific skill is being addressed – this is the criterion) written as levels of achievement or attainment (basic, developing, achieving, extending)

1. Artistic Process (Performing, Creating, Responding):	
Process Component Selected:	
Performance Outcome Selected:	
2. Mode of expected response	
3. Assessment materials needed	
4. Description of task through which students will demonstrate learning	
5. Description of the scoring device to be used	

Extension task: *Search the MCAs to find a comparable assessment and compare your ideas with the relevant MCA.*

Performance Domains

Performance domains are different than **cognitive domains,** and there are several domains to consider (Russell & Airasian, 2008): (a) communication skills (written, oral, gestural, graphic), (b) psychomotor skills, (c) athletic skills, (d) concept acquisition, and (e) affective skills. In music, communication skills are used when students announce musical works during recitals, develop program notes, give presentations, or write descriptive papers, essays, or reflections, but might also be seen as part of expressive musical communication as well. Psychomotor skills include small motor skills, such as holding instruments, bowing techniques, and fingerings, and are an essential part of musical learning. Larger motor skills, such as athletic activities, might be seen through Dalcroze movement, on the marching band field, or through dance. Concept acquisition in music may be demonstrated when students perform an expressive marking on the music though their performance, play softly in response to a conductor's *piano* gesture, identify the correct reed for their clarinet, or know how to connect speakers to an amplifier. Affective skills in music include collaborating in ensembles, responding to music, and maintaining music room behaviors/etiquettes.

Using Performance Assessments

Generally, performance assessments can be used formatively to guide both learner and teachers. Performance assessments should provide adequate information about achievement to enable students to recognize how they are progressing throughout their coursework. When used formatively, performance assessments support students to understand how they are progressing during instruction. Formative assessments may not impact an overall course grade but can be used to identify where students need assistance and feedback. When performance assessments are used summatively, at the end of a period of instruction, the intention is to summarize the learning and other accomplishments of students in a way the illustrates the extent to which a student has learned cumulatively over the period of instruction. Summative performance assessments provide a summary of a student's knowledge and skills.

Performance assessments allow for a collection of performance tasks that illustrate students' musical processes *and* their final product. Performance assessments should represent the important concepts and outcomes in the music curricula and should be planned to measure the extent to which students understand and can apply content that has been taught. Performance assessments and scoring devices can be standardized within a program so that teachers can identify their learners' strengths and weaknesses. Performance assessments however, are not easily standardized across classrooms, to those of other teachers because there is an obvious

Learning Experience: Revisit Chapter 4, Table 4.5, to review the specificity of outcomes with a partner and discuss how performance domains might be different to the domains described in Chapter 4. Complete this table for additional outcomes, in addition to the one selected in 6.1 Learning Experience.

Learning Outcomes (SWBAT...)	Response Mode	Assessment Materials	Description of the task	Description of the scoring device
Explain how responses to music are informed by the structure and the use of the elements of music.				
Describe how selected music connects to, and is influenced by, specific interests, experiences, purposes, or contexts				
Recognize the A and B sections of a composition				
Generate musical ideas within a given tonality or meter				
Use standard notation to document personal rhythmic, melodic, and simple harmonic musical ideas				

limit to the comparisons teachers can make between their students and programs. For example, the performance assessment that one teacher uses for their eighth-grade students only reflects the context of that music program and the particular skills of those students, not any other eighth-grade class. Teachers should ensure that the way they deliver or administer their performance assessments with their students is as consistent as possible, allowing students equal opportunity to illustrate their skills.

Portfolios as Performance Assessments

Portfolios are considered performance assessments because they also represent a collection of tasks that allow students to illustrate their developmental processes and final products. Portfolios are a "collection of items that document the professional trajectory or performance of a person in a particular field" (Jimenéz, 2018, p. 1264). When effectively developed, they exhibit authentic demonstrations of music learning, reflective of the outcomes expected. Portfolios are authentic assessments because in music, professional musicians are expected to have a portfolio that illustrates their professional "trajectory or performance." There are four categories into which portfolio attributes can be categorized: structure, format, types of evidence, and the scoring procedure (Jimenéz, 2018). The structure of a portfolio can span from flexible to tightly structured. When the purpose of the portfolio is to assess only learning outcomes, then the instructions for students should be general, indicating the criteria for choosing work to include (for example, chronologic or specific content) and require that it clearly demonstrates their learning. On the other hand, when portfolios are used to illustrate development of beliefs, opinions, or reflections, students are asked to add their own labels to indicate which of their thoughts go with which pieces of work or artifacts (Jimenéz, 2018). The format of a portfolio is dependent on the expectations and the works/artifacts that are found within. For example, a visual art portfolio may not contain the actual artwork but may have initial sketches and photos of the final product (Jimenéz, 2018). Likewise, music portfolios may include recordings, or perhaps video clips, especially if an electronic portfolio format is chosen. Music portfolios might also have analyses of musical pieces or studies, practice logs, self- and peer-reflections of achievement, and recordings of solos and individual performance. There is no limit for what can be included in a portfolio – various forms of media, reflections, individual work, group work, and works-in-progress such as drafts or practice session recordings. Electronic portfolios can save time by reducing paperwork and are easily contributed to, edited, reviewed, and accessed by both learner and teacher. The types of evidence included in portfolios should be varied and should cover the outcomes or competencies set by the teacher. For example, students might include not only a completed worksheet (created by the teacher to meet the objective *define an eighth note, identify eighth notes, classify eighth notes, label eighth notes*) but also their reflection of what they have learned from the learning activity and how this learning may have impacted other work, such as subsequent worksheets or music performances.

The scoring procedures for a portfolio usually include a scoring guide or rubric that defines the specific criteria for the portfolio outcomes (Jimenéz, 2018). Typically, the scoring device should include criteria specific to the quality of the artifacts submitted (if they had not been evaluated prior to being included in the portfolio). If artifacts have not been scored prior to inclusion in the portfolio, then each artifact should have its own scoring guide. For example, a performance rubric for a musical performance recording or answer key for multiple-choice tests. When artifacts have been previously scored (with appropriate scoring devices specific to each artifact) then the quality of the task is based on the overall evidence submitted. The criteria for considering the purpose of the portfolio may focus on how the student defined their learning through their selection of artifacts and descriptive reflections. Multiple forms of evidence may be included in a portfolio, which should allow the learner to illustrate or justify their learning. Reflection is an important component of portfolios and learners should be encouraged to firstly collect artifacts, then select the most meaningful artifacts, then connect the artifacts as part of their learning by reflecting on the inclusion of each artifact. Figure 6.1 provides an example.

Burrack (2002) suggests that students take more ownership of their musical learning and develop a greater awareness of their music when they undertake portfolio assessments. There are several uses of portfolios, and Hill (2008) suggests three that offer unique opportunities for music educators: learning (formative), assessment (summative), and employment (marketing or showcase). The formative use is an ongoing support of student learning development, whereas the summative portfolio formally evaluates overall development of learning outcomes. Marketing portfolios may be used as more senior music students seek to share their musical works with prospective colleges as part of admission and application processes.

There are some drawbacks with portfolios. Portfolio assessments can be time-consuming for both students and teachers, and there are difficulties with scoring them (Jimenéz, 2018). Rater reliability is an issue with portfolio scoring, most notably when used for high-stakes tests, and there is an additional challenge for scorers to balance the quality of the artifacts with the way the connections between artifacts are illustrated. Jimenez notes that reliability issues can be mediated if teachers, when engaging in classroom uses of portfolio assessments, engage in double scoring to compare scores between more than one rater and gauge rater reliability. Portfolios allow students to illustrate both what they know and how they know, by submitting statements about their learning, with authentic work samples as support. As a performance assessment, portfolios allow for standards-based assessment of student learning in a wide variety of music classrooms.

☐   **Tests (select 2 or more to include)**
      ☐   Aural
      ☐   History
      ☐   Musical vocabulary and term recognition
☐   Summary of learning on tests and reflection of where I need to improve

☐   **Assignments (select 2 or more to include)**
      ☐   Log of listening habits
      ☐   Interview with parents about their favorite music
      ☐   Theory assignment – intervals
      ☐   Theory assignment – key signatures
      ☐   Composition or improvisation recording
☐   Summary of learning on assignments and reflection of where I need to improve

☐   **Self-assessments (select 2 or more to include)**
      ☐   Rehearsal self-assessment
      ☐   Concert self-assessment
      ☐   Playing test –video self-assessment
      ☐   Ensemble recording – performance criteria
☐   Summary of self-assessments and reflection on what I have noticed about my playing

☐   **Audio recordings (select 2 or more to include)**
      ☐   Myself at jury
      ☐   Ensemble at festival
      ☐   Myself in solo/ensemble
      ☐   Favorite recordings
☐   Reflection about my recordings and what I have noticed

Portfolio will be evaluated with the following scoring scheme:

Level 1 – Emerging self-assessor
Does not perceive area of change or improvement despite evidence
Does not observe self in the process of improving

Level 2 – Making connections as self-assessor
Acknowledges/identifies some change to practice has occurred
Partially observes self in the process of improving

Level 3 – Reflective self-assessor
Consistently acknowledges and articulates changes occurring in practice
Observes self often in the process of improving

Figure 6.1 An example of a music portfolio designed to measure students' self-assessment of their work

In summary, performance assessments allow teachers to directly observe skills and applied knowledge in students. Performance assessments can be used formatively, at several instances to inform both the learner and the teacher, and they can be used summatively in ways that illustrate overall development. Performance assessments must be designed by teachers in ways that reflect their goals, while considering the needs and expectations of learners.

References

Burrack, F. (2002). Enhanced assessment in instrumental programs. *Music Educators Journal*, 88(6), 27–32. Retrieved from www.jstor.org/stable/3399802

Brophy, T. S. (2003). Developing and implementing standards-based assessments. In C. Lindemann (Ed.), *Benchmarks in action: A guide to standards-based assessment in music* (pp. 11–16). Reston, VA: MENC and the National Association for Music Education.

Hill, C. (2008). A portfolio model for music educators. *Music Educators Journal*, 95(1), 61–72. https://doi-org/10.1177/0027432108318481

Jimenéz, D. (2018). Portfolio assessment. In B. B. Frey (Ed.), *The Sage encyclopedia of educational research, measurement, and evaluation* (pp. 1264–1266). Thousand Oaks, CA: Sage Publications.

Lindvall, C. M. (1961). *Testing and evaluation: An introduction*. New York: Harcourt, Brace and World.

Nitko, A. J. (1996). *Educational assessment of students* (2nd ed.). Englewood Cliffs, NJ: Prentice- Hall, Inc.

Russell, M. K., & Airasian, P. W. (2008). *Classroom assessment: Concepts and applications*. New York, NY: McGraw-Hill.

7   Indirect Assessment Techniques

Frederick Burrack and Phillip Payne

Chapter Overview

Chapter 7 offers strategies to help better understand future students' experience in and throughout a music program. The assessment processes also can expose students' self-concept as a musician and learner of music and beliefs in students' ability to succeed as a musician. These approaches, while often not considered as learning assessment, could be useful to a music teacher to provide proper and effective documentation. Techniques are provided to analyze and compare findings to direct assessments, revealing learning influences that can guide instructional and curricular decisions.

Learning Expectations for the Chapter

- Understand the difference between direct and indirect assessments.
- Recognize the value of indirect assessment to confirm the quality of student learning.
- Develop student self- and peer-assessments that can enhance student learning.
- Create journal prompts that can effectively develop and expose improved learning.
- Plan a structure for focus groups.

Essential Questions for the Chapter

- In what ways might direct assessment be insufficient to fully understand the quality of student learning?
- How do self- and peer-assessments improve student learning?
- How can talking with students in a focus group become a form of assessment?
- What strategies exist to use indirect assessment to guide instruction and curriculum development?

What Are Indirect Assessments?

It is important for all educators to understand the difference between direct and indirect evidence of student learning and their individual purposes within an assessment process. Direct assessment is observable and measurable evidence of student learning (Center for Teaching and Learning, 2019). These are typically the foundation for instructional decisions made by music teachers. Students' involvement in the artistic processes of performing, creating, and responding provides compelling evidence of what music students have and have not learned within the music classroom.

Indirect evidence often consists of indicators of students' attitudes and beliefs toward learning. Examples of indirect evidence can come from discussions with students individually or in groups, feedback from other students such as a section leader or other peers, and questionnaires or surveys asking students to self-report what they have learned.

Although music teachers can easily identify ways in which students can demonstrate music learning, indirect evidence of learning is less clear. For example, while students submit work to demonstrate what they have learned, the music teacher may not ever see the work in the student's personal context or have an opportunity to evaluate it.

Indirect assessments can provide valuable insights into student experiences in the program, as well as students' perceptions of learning. They can provide information as to experiential impact of instruction, aspects of the educational experience that students would like revised or added, and challenges that students have encountered in sequence and/or expectation. When music educators move beyond their own feelings of programmatic appropriateness, instructional sequence, musical content, and performance achievement, indirect assessments may expose aspects of student learning and their experience that can enhance instructional processes leading toward higher levels of achievement. They also may provide inferential evidence as to why students persist in or leave the music program, choices made by students as they progress in the program, enrollment trends, and diversity of students in the program. These types of data provide evidence about a program and challenges hindering program success.

How Does a Music Teacher Determine Whether an Assessment Measure of Learning Is Direct Evidence or a Proxy for Learning?

Examples of direct evidence of learning include students' completed work as assigned or a performance meeting a specific level as defined by the learning outcome. Indirect evidence of learning might come from identifying whether students have participated in a learning activity, their opinions about what they have learned, reported student satisfaction, or peer-and self-assessments of tasks throughout the learning process. Students and/ or peers can rate their learning of specific concepts or critique other students' performances or skill sets. Tools to gain this type of information often come from peer evaluations, surveys that ask students how much they have learned, students scoring themselves, or overall course grades. Course grades, although based on a collection of direct measurements, can be considered indirect measures of learning because (a) they represent a combination of course learning outcomes, (b) frequently include additional components not related to learning outcomes, such as extra credit, participation, or penalties for unexcused absences, and (c) averages of multiple scores resulting in the inability to differentiate achievement from challenges.

Indirect measures provide valuable information that can support direct assessment evidence of learning or provide insight to learning not attainable through the direct measure. Indirect measures are valid forms of assessment given their intended use. Validity resides in the function to provide context to student experience. When compared with data from direct assessments, they are extremely useful tools in providing a comprehensive view of student learning. When comparing findings from indirect assessments to those from direct assessments, the understanding of student learning may take on a different meaning. For example, indirect assessments may discover that students do not recognize their own progress or achievements. Conversely, students can often overinflate their capabilities, hindering their motivation to practice or achieve at higher levels. Another possible finding as a result of indirect assessments is identifying when a student accurately recognizes their achievement level but does not feel confident in their ability to progress further. It is important to identify how students feel about their achievement, progress, or ability to improve in order to provide effective instruction and create a conducive environment for learning.

Another example of an indirect assessment is when a peer evaluates and provides feedback to another student. How the student interacts with the peer feedback would be an indirect assessment of conceptual understanding and musical performance. In this instance, however, this assessment would also be direct evidence of the student reviewer's analytical, evaluative, and possibly problem-solving skills. In addition, if the peer review is in written form, it could be direct assessment of written communication skills. Peer assessments are extremely useful as a teaching and learning tool to develop listening, analysis, problem-solving, evaluative, and goal-setting skills. They require a high level of student involvement in observing, investigating, drawing inferences from data, and/or forming hypotheses. These aspects of music learning are essential in fostering effective musicianship, and the peer assessment could be an effective way to provide direct evidence for the peer assessor as well as an indirect measure of performance proficiency for the student being assessed. These forms of assessments are integrated into each of the MCAs aligned with the 2014 National Standards.

Methods of Indirect Assessment

Indirect assessment methods require that music educators infer actual student abilities, knowledge, and values rather than observe direct evidence (Skidmore, 2019), as long as it is clearly understood that they provide supportive evidence of learning and are not hard evidence of learning or achievement. Advantages of indirect assessment methods include:

- Providing clues about what could be assessed directly.
- Exposing areas of learning, attitudes, and experiences that direct assessments cannot capture.
- Usefulness for ascertaining values and beliefs.

The remainder of this chapter will explore a variety of indirect assessment methods that are appropriate for a music classroom.

Student Self-Assessment

Student self-assessment involves students in evaluating their own work, skills, and achievement of learning goals. This assessment, as an activity, increases students' awareness of learning progress and reveals insight into gaps in learning. As an assessment, it would be considered an indirect measure of performance skills, but there are components of self-assessment that are direct measures of learning. Self-assessments are a direct measure of students' awareness of their own learning progress. Integrating self-assessment throughout music learning promotes student ownership of musical development, which is foundational for setting goals, practicing, and performance achievement. As a music learning activity, self-assessment develops the skills of listening, self-critiquing, and evaluating in order to identify musical problems and develop pedagogical and musical solutions to challenges. All musicians from beginning to professional level should possess the skills to evaluate their own performance. Therefore, this practice should be embedded in music learning as early as possible as an instructional activity and as a form of assessment.

Teachers who effectively integrate student self-assessment and peer-assessment do so in a sequence that begins early in the curriculum. A student's first experience with self-assessment works best when initiated as a group process that then proceeds to individual self-assessment. In the second-grade MCA, self-assessment is included whereby students listening to their own singing answer questions about their performance by circling appropriate icons (see the Second Grade MCA for Performing,

p. 9). This MCA includes peer-assessment when students provide verbal feedback to help their peers improve. In the fifth-grade General Music MCA, after gaining feedback from their teacher or peers, students self-evaluate their skills as they prepare for their final performance (see the Fifth Grade MCA for Performing, p. 14). In the Ensemble MCAs at all levels, self-assessments are included as practice logs with peer-assessment interjected to guide improvements before the final summative assessment. Inherent in all levels of the creating MCAs, students assess their work as they develop the projects.

> *Learning Experience:* Write a critical review of an MCA for Performing, discussing your opinion as to its appropriateness, thoroughness, and applicability of self-assessment for a music class that you would teach.

In many ensemble classrooms, students are asked to record portions of lesson books/etudes/ensemble/solo pieces and then listen to the recorded performance. Students are often provided with a scoring rubric as an assessment tool to focus on concepts such as rhythm, pitch and tone, technique, and expressive musicianship. As the students listen critically to their performance, they write their observations on the scoring rubric and make suggestions for improvement in each category (see Figure 7.1).

With improvement of student learning serving as the primary purpose of assessment, it is important for the music educator to provide immediate feedback concerning the quality of the performance. Feedback enhances the students' understanding of their self-observations and guides decisions in how to improve their self-assessment abilities. Music learning through self-assessment has been explored in ARTS Propel (Davidson, Ross-Broadus, Charlton, Scripp, & Waanders, 1992) and many articles since (Goolsby, 1999; Hale & Green, 2009; Burrack, 2002; Crochet & Green, 2012; DeLuca & Bolden, 2014; Valle, Andrade, Palma, & Hefferen, 2016). Self-assessment is an opportunity for students to set improvement goals that become the focus for individual practice. As a means of assessment, students and their teachers periodically refer to completed self- and peer-assessment forms as well as their performance assessments to determine progress toward or achievement of stated goals (see Figure 7.2).

An effective assessment process should gradually increase the depth and quality of student self-assessment throughout the entire curriculum. Teachers at each level in any music program should integrate expectations for self-assessment with increasing expectations for analytical and

Name_____   Date_____

MUSIC PERFORMED: _____

Tone Quality *(overall control, warmth, clarity and consistency)*

Pitch Accuracy and Intonation *(accuracy and intonation of all pitches in all registers)*

Rhythmic Accuracy *(steadiness of beat and accuracy of the printed rhythms)*

Musical Interpretation *(musicianship and presentation of musical ideas such as phrasing, tempo, style, and dynamics)*

Articulation and Technique *(precision of marked articulations and appropriate interpretations of markings)*

Goals for Personal Improvement *(specific ways that you can improve upon any aspect covered above and how you can personally contribute more to the large group setting)*

Figure 7.1 Self-assessment example

problem-solving skills. These self-assessments provide direct evidence of analytical and problem-solving skills, in addition to indirect evidence of performance skills. It is typical in the high school years for students to self-assess technical skills within excerpts from the music studied in class each quarter of the academic year. As seen in the ensemble MCAs, when students feel prepared and record the required selections, they are

Assessment strategy:
Using the video or audio tape of a performance, have the students listen to themselves and evaluate the performance for: Tone Quality; Rhythmic Accuracy; Intonation; Balance and Blend; Technical Accuracy; and Musical Interpretation. There should be at least one description in each category, (similar to a large group contest evaluation). Keep the evaluations in the student's portfolio to compare improvements in listening and assessments with future evaluations.

Description of basic level student response:
1. The descriptions in the evaluations are written in complete sentences.
2. The student describes technical imperfections in the performance. Although problems are identified, specific descriptions of measure numbers and rhythmic placement is lacking.
3. The descriptions use musical terminology.
4. Descriptions of balance uses words such as: "Trumpets are too loud", "the clarinets are out of tune"
5. Analyzations are centered around technical proficiency and lacking in tonal quality and musical interpretation.

Description of proficient level student response:
1. The student identifies successes as well as problems in the performance.
2. Specific placement of problems are identified.
3. Terminology such as: "Depth of tone", "The clarinets kept their tone dark in the lyrical section", "The clarinets need to adjust their intonation bringing their highest tone up to the center of the pitch"; identifying specific solutions.
4. Expressive elements are identified with terminology such as crescendo, rallentando, etc.

Description of advanced level student response:
1. The student begins to share feeling they have in relation to the performance. "The crescendo in the trumpet section after E gave me goose bumps", "The climax of the piece was expressed well in the low brass section".
2. The student annualization is so complete that there is not enough space supplied for this evaluation.
3. The student identifies cadences, harmonic tension, and makes comparison to historical genre of the composition.
4. The student spends more time on expressive elements than on technical proficiency.

Figure 7.2 Self-assessment scoring device

asked to assess themselves to guide further rehearsal and improvement until the final presentation that will be scored by the teacher. In this MCA, the music teacher provides constructive feedback to the students using a rubric scoring device.

Learning Experience: Select a music class and grade level for which to develop an assignment that includes student self-assessment. Include the following:

- Assignment title and general description of the assessment task.
- Expected learning outcomes.
- Prerequisite knowledge and skills.
- Teacher preparation and materials.
- Step-by-step assessment sequence.
- Scoring devices to be used.

Peer-Assessment

Developing sensitivity in listening skills, exposing awareness of musical concepts in performances, and improvement in analytical skills that can guide performance improvement is often attained in a *peer-assessment*. This is when a student assesses the performance of an individual peer or a larger group of peers. Nearly all of the MCAs include students asking peers to provide feedback on performance, composition, or other projects. The MCAs provide a structured form to guide students' focus as they provide feedback to their peer and guide the student performer/composer to make critical decisions as to which feedback to incorporate or disregard.

Learning Experience: Write a critical review of an MCA that includes peer-assessment; discuss your opinion as to its appropriateness, thoroughness, and applicability for a music class that you would teach.

Since a similar process of evaluation is a part of regional or state large group evaluation (often called festival or all-state), using the familiar ballot for peer-assessment enables music students to experience these performance expectations in the music class. Using a recording of their ensemble from a recent rehearsal, having students evaluate the ensemble can be an effective measure for developing and assessing listening and analytical skills. If using a form similar to what was seen in Figure 7.1, teachers might consider altering the final section from "Goals for Personal Improvement" to "General Feedback for Improvement." An advantage of group peer-assessment is increasing students' awareness of how a judge will be evaluating them in future musical experiences, such as those often included in a school music festival or at auditions. It is appropriate to prepare the students for this type of evaluation by teaching them to assess each other. This assessment process works well if scattered throughout rehearsals over the weeks of preparation for concerts or contests. As suggested by Burrack (2002),

> Students are encouraged to (a) listen for specific elements of tone quality, intonation, rhythm, balance and blend, technique, interpretation, and articulation, and (b) write at least one specific observation in each category on the assessment sheet. Immediately following the assessment, the students share their comments and suggestions. When the students verbally offer their suggestions for improvement and immediately apply these suggestions by performing the selection, they gain independence and self-direction in the learning process and exhibit an enhanced performance quality.
>
> (p. 28)

Learning Experience: Select a music class and grade level for which to develop a scoring device to be used for an assignment that includes peer-assessment. Include the following:

- Assignment title and general description of the assessment task.
- Expected learning outcomes.
- Scoring devices that address all learning expectations for the peer-assessment.

Journaling

Since affective development is as important in music learning as is cognitive learning, student journals are an effective tool for music teachers to examine student learning in both the affective and cognitive domains. If approached as an opportunity for thoughtful reflection of their music learning, journaling can provide a nonthreatening process for students to communicate their knowledge and feelings about their performance skills, development of learning outcomes, and attitudes about the music studied.

Allowing the students to journal helps them identify the challenges, set goals for personal improvement, document discovered aspects within the music, or share feelings elicited from the musical experience. The most important learning that occurs from journaling is activating thought processes through which students analyze what they hear and feel. Developing journal prompts that reflect your course or PLOs are critical in the initial planning stages of journal use. To use journaling as a means of assessment, a scoring device should be employed to identify qualities of the expected learning. As a means of assessment, a journal will not confirm the attainment of performance skills but will expose aspects of student learning outcomes not easily observable such as self-efficacy, aesthetic response, professional attitudes, and effective listening skills.

The following examples of journal prompts provide a few ideas that encourage deeper considerations of experience in a music class:

Critical Listening
- Identify two areas you wish to improve during your sectional tomorrow morning identifying two strategies on how you plan to rehearse each area.

Expressivity
- Draw a picture (or tell a story) expressing your understanding of the moments in (the music).

Emotional Connection
- Music often brings back memories and the feelings associated with memories. Identify in any portion of a piece studied in class that reminds you of a certain time in your life and explain why this particular song brings back those memories (freely adapted from Tanner, 2019).

Connection to Text
- Song lyrics can express emotions, such as love or sorrow. What piece from our music clearly communicates a particular emotion? Explain why the lyrics from that piece represent feeling.

Historical Context
- William Congreve (1670–1729) was an English playwright and poet who wrote, "Music hath charms to soothe a savage beast." Write about a point in one of the pieces studied that touches you emotionally or positively impacts your attitude.

Learning Experience: Develop a journaling assignment appropriate for a music class of your choice. This assignment should include the following:

- Type of music class and age of students.
- Intended learning outcome and rationale as to how asking students to think more deeply will enhance student learning related to this outcome.
- Journal prompt you feel will elicit deeper consideration for students.
- Scoring device to be used with this assignment.
- Which aspects might be considered direct evidence of learning and which aspects provide indirect indicators?

Focus Groups

It is common for music teachers to meet with students, but such a meeting is not often utilized as a form of indirect assessment. Interviews and focus groups allow teachers to talk with students and ask important questions face-to-face. When a music teacher wants to intentionally explore important issues and maintains notes on findings and discoveries, focus groups become important as a means of assessment. Using focus groups to gather information on student experience allows music teachers to identify effective instructional processes that are perceived as impacting learning and can reveal aspects of student experience that may hinder development and attitude. Since student expectations are a moving target, it is important to stay abreast of students' perspectives. Determining when to use focus groups should be part of student learning assessment, as well as program assessment (see Chapter 9), and can be used to guide curricular content, sequence, instructional planning, and goal setting. Focus groups can be intentionally scheduled throughout an academic year as a proactive assessment strategy or organized when issues occur as a reactive assessment. Focus groups can also be considered a strand of action-research.

What Are the Different Types of Focus Groups?

Music teachers can use focus groups to provide evidence or develop understanding for most any question. Possible topics could focus on performance quality, student experience and attitude, goals for improvement, or uncovering potential issues. A well-planned focus group with clear objectives can help develop and refine the answers. The following are a few examples of focus groups issues:

- If there appears to be a trend across a music class or program of a skill or knowledge deficiency, focus groups are useful in assessing whether students recognize an issue. It is useful to gain their perceptions as to what might influence the issue and possible causes. Selecting participants of focus groups by cohort criteria may provide different views.
- Asking students about the extent to which they have progressed in each learning outcome may expose internalized motivations or attitudes not evident in student performance. It is always good to request supportive evidence for their perceptions as well as gain alternate understandings of intended learning outcomes.

How Many Students Should Participate in a Focus Group?

The whole point of selecting participants of a focus group is to elicit as many different perspectives as possible. Too many students can impede ideas from many participants. Too few participants will limit perspectives due to inhibitions of students involved. The ideal size group is eight to ten students depending on the topic. Selecting focus group participants should be based on their familiarity with the issue and expectation for a variety of perspectives. It may also be useful to organize three or four different groups to ensure that what is exposed allows for multiple perspectives.

Techniques for Managing a Focus Group

The most important first step is to identify the specific issue or focus for organizing the group. Some ideas might fall in the following assessment categories:

- Identify student recognition of a problem and attain their ideas and leadership to solve the issue.
- Assess the effectiveness of specific instructional strategies.
- Expose attitudes toward a new idea or direction for the program.
- Confirm the extent of learning for a learning outcome.

A second step is to target the students who could expose aspects of the issue, e.g., students within a grade or skill level, students who have demonstrated leadership, or students demonstrating challenges. It is important not to select a focus group to confirm your beliefs or observations, but to gain understanding of a problem or issue that may not be fully recognized or understood.

The next step is to plan questions that will initiate student discussion without guiding their response. It is generally best to ask open-ended questions that require specific examples rather than agreement. Planning only a few key questions with possible follow-up questions is usually a good strategy. In a focus group it is important to encourage students to share openly. Students will always be aware of you as their teacher, so it is important to consider that students might be intimidated toward the way they perceive you want them to answer. If this might be the case, you could consider having someone other than yourself lead the focus group, such as a student leader or assistant music director. During the focus group, a good idea is to enable the students to recognize that their ideas are important for making improvements. Introduce the question and let the students share their ideas without imposing your own, although clarifying your understanding of their thoughts is very important. Questions such as "Am I understanding that you think . . ." or "What I am hearing is . . ." might be helpful for you to clarify. Be alert for students who dominate the conversation. It will be important to ask others for their opinions and ensure all students have an opportunity to speak. If possible, record the conversation, with the permission of the students, if you might later want to revise the information or to make use of the data as an assessment.

Sample Questions You Might Consider

1. There are several learning goals that we hope everyone will attain in this course. One of the learning outcomes is _____. We would like everyone to share where you are in your progress in this outcome and your personal achievement goal.
2. What challenge have you experienced in your learning for this outcome?
3. What assignment or learning experience was most useful in helping you achieve your goal in this outcome?
4. If you could give any advice to improve this class, what would it be?
5. What other issues would you like to discuss?

The most important result of any focus group is to recognize aspects of student learning, impact of instruction, or effectiveness of curriculum or receive guidance for future decisions. If the focus group is centered around important issues, the collection and analysis of responses to guide curricular and instructional decisions can become a valued assessment for your program. A focus group becomes most useful when teachers discover aspects about what students understand or value, and this helps the teacher understand the program in ways that may not be easily observed or otherwise measured.

Learning Experience: Identify a question that you could pursue in a focus group about a learning expectation for a class, ensemble, or music organization. Identify a cohort of stakeholders and lead a focus group to explore student conceptions, beliefs, or experiences relating to the learning outcome. Compile the results into discoveries. The report should include:

- The learning outcome and question intended to be pursued.
- The guiding questions used in the focus group.
- Summary of student responses.

Describe why the responses are considered indirect indicators of learning.

Surveys

Music teachers seldom think of asking students questions via a survey, but short, focused surveys can provide valuable information about many issues. Advantages of surveys include (a) information is simultaneously attained from all students; (b) opinions about the program can be easily accessed; (c) critiques can be attained of activities or practices; and (d) provision of a current view pertaining to the impact of learning. Since student opinions may change over time, periodic surveys are often useful.

Student surveys are easy to administer in paper form, although this can result in an extra work for the music teacher to collect, sort, and analyze the data. Using a web-based tool, survey administration (delivery) is automatic. With the tediousness relieved using a web-based survey platform, there are few reasons not to use this form of indirect assessment. A primary concern with any survey is response rate; therefore, it is critical to keep them concise and focused. You should only ask for information that is important to both you and your students.

In designing questions, it is probably useful to ask a variety of questions types such as Likert-scale questions (e.g., Totally Agree 1 . . . 2 . . . 3 . . . 4 . . . 5 . . . 6 . . . 7 Totally Disagree) and attitudinal questions (e.g., Strongly Agree, Agree, Disagree, Strongly Disagree). Other types of questions include:

> Single-answer questions: This type of forced-choice question asks students to select one from a set of predesigned responses. Because these types of questions allow only a limited number of responses, they are best for when the music teacher wants to know information about specific issues.
>
> How much progress do you feel you have made in accurately sight-reading?
> ❑ None   ❑ Little   ❑ Some   ❑ A great deal
>
> Multi-select questions: Instead of asking for a single response, these questions typically are in the form of a set of check boxes. The student has set of predefined choices but can select more than one option. In a self-report survey such as this, it is important to inform the students that they can select all that apply.
>
> I am confident in my ability to:
> ❑ Define the meaning of musical terminology.
> ❑ Recognize historical periods of music.
> ❑ Sing most melodies in solfège syllables.
> ❑ Compose a melody and two variations.
> ❑ Perform a solo in front of an audience.
> ❑ Research data for program notes.
>
> Ranking: Ranking questions ask students to compare different issues to one another (e.g., "Please rank each of the following items in order of importance with #1 being the most important and #6

being the least important.") An example of a ranking question would be:

> Think across the current school year and rank the following assignments in the order of most important (1) for development of your performance skills to least important (6) by placing 1–6 on the line provided.
>
> ___ Studying a solo.
> ___ Performing in an ensemble.
> ___ Listening to music.
> ___ Playing scales.
> ___ Reading through etudes.
> ___ Researching information about musical pieces/ composers.

Rating: Rating questions ask students to rate different items using a common scale. For example:

> Rate the level of competence you have, by checking the boxes, in the following learning outcomes:

Outcome

	Beginner	. . . .	Intermediate	. . . .	Proficient
Sight-reading	❑	❑	❑	❑	❑
Musical Expression	❑	❑	❑	❑	❑
Articulation/Diction	❑	❑	❑	❑	❑
Rhythmic Accuracy	❑	❑	❑	❑	❑
Performance Skills	❑	❑	❑	❑	❑

Open-ended questions: Open-ended questions do not offer answer choices and typically begin with "what" or "why." They are designed to elicit an instinctive response and provide qualitative information. Be sure to allow space for students to write their answers in paper-based forms or, alternatively, use an online platform such as Google Survey or one within your school learning management system (such as Google Classroom, Canvas, Moodle, Schoology, Desire2Learn [D2L], or Brightspace). Examples of open-ended questions:

> Describe the most difficult challenge that you encountered this year in the music program.
> If you had time to redo one of your performances, which would it be and what would you do differently?

Other elements you might consider to guide question decisions for surveys include:
• Rate your satisfaction with . . .
• How confident are you in your ability to . . .?

- How much has your experience in this class contributed to your ability to . . .?
- During the current year, how often have you . . .?
- Looking back at your experience in this class, should less, the same, or more emphasis be placed on . . .?
- How much progress have you made in . . .?

Learning Experience: Create a five-question survey for music education majors at your institution focused on student perceptions as to their learning development of outcomes in a university ensemble. Use at least three types of questions. Include a survey title and description that will entice students to complete and a description of each learning outcome.

Alternative Experience: Create a survey for a music program regarding the scheduling of performances and other events for the upcoming school year.

Alternative Experience: Create a survey for a music booster club to identify their goals for the program, their attitudes toward current levels of support, and their understanding of your goals.

Summary: Using Indirect Assessment Data

Indirect assessments can be extremely useful to understand student conception of learning, self-efficacy, and self-confidence as a musician. The relationship a student has with the educational experience with music is as important as the development of skills and knowledge.

In conclusion, think about what you can understand about student learning from indirect assessments by completing Table 7.1 to explore the value and challenges of indirect assessment in a school music program.

Table 7.1 Value and weaknesses of indirect assessments

Potential Value of Indirect Assessments	Potential Weaknesses of Indirect Assessment

Summative Activity: *You are curious why there is such an achievement gap within your students in a future classroom. Use the template below to develop an assessment plan that might indicate possible causes.*

Course:	*Select a hypothetical course; what course do you see yourself teaching in your first job?*
Questions:	*What questions about student learning and experiences will provide context for future curricular decisions?* *1)* *2)* *3)*
Indirect Assessments:	*List 2–3 indirect assessments you could use to attain data to answer these questions.* *1)* *2)* *3)*
Scoring:	*[Provide the scoring device and anticipated analysis plan.]*
Assessment Plan:	*[Develop a plan to administer these assessments throughout the curriculum.]*

References

Burrack, F. (2002). Enhanced assessment in instrumental programs. *Music Educator's Journal, 88*(6), 27–32.

Center for Teaching and Learning. (2019). *Direct versus indirect assessment of student learning.* [Online tutorial]. Retrieved from https://resources.depaul.edu/teaching-commons/teaching-guides/feedback-grading/Pages/direct-assessment.aspx

Crochet, L., & Green, S. (2012). Examining progress across time with practical assessments in ensemble settings. *Music Educators Journal, 98*(3), 49–54.

Davidson, L., Ross-Broadus, L., Charlton, J., Scripp, L., & Waanders, J. (1992). *Arts PROPEL: A handbook for music.* Cambridge, MA: Project Zero, Harvard Graduate School of Education.

DeLuca, C., & Bolden, B. (2014). Music performance assessment: Exploring three approaches for quality rubric construction. *Music Educators Journal, 101*(1), 70–76. https://doi.org/10.1177/0027432114540336

Goolsby, T. (1999). Assessment in instrumental music. *Music Educators Journal, 86*(2), 31–35.

Hale, C., & Green, S. (2009). Six key principles for music assessment. *Music Educators Journal, 95*(4), 27–31.

Skidmore Institutional Assessment. (2019). *Indirect assessment methods.* Retrieved from www.skidmore.edu/assessment/archived/indirect-assessment-methods.php

Tanner, S. (2019). *Music journals 1–8*. Retrieved April 22, 2019 from http:// tanner-musicappreciation.weebly.com/music-journal-questions.html

Valle, C., Andrade, H., Palma, M., & Hefferen, J. (2016). Applications of peer assessment and self-assessment in music. *Educational & Counseling Psychology Faculty Scholarship*, *11*. Retrieved April 22, 2019 from http://scholars archive.library.albany.edu/edpsych_fac_scholar/11

8 Analyzing Classroom Assessment Data

Brian C. Wesolowski

Chapter Overview

This chapter focuses on how to describe and analyze classroom testing data, with the intent of informing future teaching and learning processes and improving future test uses from both a class-centered perspective and an individual student-centered perspective. Concepts covered include item- and person-ordering, item difficulty, person ability, item- and person-discrimination, and distractor analyses.

Learning Expectations for the Chapter

- Examine the relationship between person ability and item difficulty.
- Calculate and evaluate item difficulty and person ability.
- Calculate and evaluate item- and person-discrimination.
- Use distractor analyses to better understand abnormalities in the outcome testing data.

Essential Questions for the Chapter

- How can learning outcome data be used in a way that informs teaching and learning while also communicating to administrators the types and quality of teaching and learning occurring in the music classroom?
- How do I calculate item difficulty and item-discrimination indices?
- How can item difficulty and item-discrimination indices inform class-centered learning outcomes?
- How do I calculate person ability and person-discrimination indices?
- How can person ability and person-discrimination indices inform student-centered learning outcomes?
- How do distractor analyses provide more meaningful insight into response patterns?

Today's educational environment is becoming increasingly data-driven, and there is a clear need to communicate to administrators and other educational stakeholders the teaching and learning occurring in music classrooms using empirical data (Wesolowski, 2014, 2015). As discussed in Chapter 5, the literature pertaining to the procedural and analytical methods for demonstrating student achievement is most often in the context of large-scale, standardized tests. However, 69% of classroom educators, including music educators, instruct students in a discipline where they are not evaluated in the context of standardized testing (National Comprehensive Center for Teacher Quality, 2011). For these 69% of educators, it becomes their responsibility to communicate to stakeholders the representative student achievement in their classrooms using classroom assessments. From a music education perspective, this can be even more daunting, as administrators and stakeholders are not often familiar with teaching and learning processes specific to the field of music (Hart, 2003). Therefore, it is critical for music educators to provide data from assessments that validly, reliably, and fairly represent the true teaching and learning within the music classroom in a way that administrators and stakeholders can understand. This chapter reviews procedures to generate, collect, and disseminate data in a way that can provide empirical evidence of music student achievement in meaningful ways while generating empirical evidence to make informed inferences related to the quality of the test itself.

Setting the Stage

Let us suppose that a music educator teaches a unit to their general music class on instrument timbre. One part of the teacher's overall assessment is to provide a multiple-choice listening test with 20 samples of music, highlighting various performances of instruments discussed in the unit. For each musical sample played, the students are asked to select which musical instrument is performing from one of four choices using a sound-to-picture multiple-choice format. As an example, for Item 1, the student would be prompted with pictures of a piano, clarinet, trumpet, and timpani. The teacher would play an example of a solo piano sonata, and the student would answer the item correctly by circling a picture of the piano.

The teacher will rely on the results of the test as one part of the overall student assessment in order to observe how successful the instructional delivery was and to identify how well the students have learned to aurally identify various instrument timbres. Based upon what the teacher knows about the students from the class interactions, some musical samples were selected because they were considered relatively easy to identify and it is anticipated that most students would correctly identify the instrument. Other musical samples were selected because they were considered to

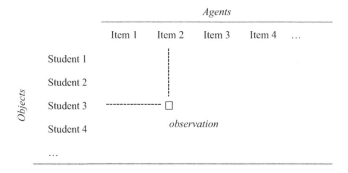

Figure 8.1 A representation of an observation stemming from the interaction between one object (Student 3) and one agent (Item 2)

be relatively difficult and only students possessing higher levels of aural discrimination would be able to correctly identify the instrument. Other musical selections sit somewhere in the middle, where it is anticipated that that some students would correctly identify the instrument while others would not.

There are two important outcomes that can be drawn from this testing context. The first piece of information is the expected ordering of the students from highest ability to the lowest ability. In this instance, the students are considered to be the *objects* of the testing context because they are being evaluated. The second piece of information is the expected ordering of the test items from the most difficult to the least difficult. In this instance, the items are considered to be the *agents* of the testing context because they are doing the evaluating. Throughout the testing process, each object (i.e., student) interacts with each agent (i.e., item). Each of these interactions is referred to as a raw score response, or an *observation* (see Figure 8.1). The considerations toward the ordering of objects, the ordering of agents, and all the individual observations provide a teacher with the overall picture of the testing context. It is the music educator's job to then evaluate, interpret, and diagnose the truthfulness of the outcomes. The teacher needs to ask, *Do the outcomes cooperate with my intentions and expectations behind the test while also representing the true teaching and learning occurring in the classroom?*

Constructing a Data Matrix and Right/Wrong Matrix

The observations for the hypothetical example described earlier can be found in the data matrix depicted in Table 8.1. In this example, 18 students responded to 20 multiple-choice items, resulting in a total of 360

Table 8.1 Data matrix containing raw score responses of 18 students to 21 items

		Agents																			
Items	I01	I02	I03	I04	I05	I06	I07	I08	I09	I10	I11	I12	I13	I14	I15	I16	I17	I18	I19	I20
Correct Answers	3	1	1	1	4	1	3	3	1	3	2	1	1	2	3	2	1	1	2	2
Student 1	1	3	2	3	4	2	2	1	2	3	2	3	2	1	3	2	3	1	1	1
Student 2	3	1	3	3	2	1	2	1	1	2	2	1	1	2	1	1	1	1	2	2
Student 3	4	2	2	2	3	2	3	2	1	2	1	1	1	2	2	1	2	1	2	2
Student 4	3	1	1	1	4	1	3	3	1	3	2	1	1	2	1	2	1	1	2	2
Student 5	3	1	1	1	4	1	2	3	1	3	2	1	2	2	2	2	1	1	2	2
Student 6	1	2	3	1	2	1	2	3	1	3	2	3	1	1	3	2	3	1	1	2
Student 7	1	3	3	1	2	2	2	3	2	2	1	1	2	2	1	1	3	2	2	2
Student 8	1	2	3	3	2	3	1	3	1	2	2	2	2	2	1	2	3	1	2	1
Student 9	1	3	1	1	4	1	2	3	1	3	2	2	2	2	1	2	3	1	2	2
Student 10	3	1	3	1	2	1	3	1	1	3	2	2	1	2	2	3	3	1	2	2
Student 11	3	1	1	1	4	1	3	1	1	3	3	1	1	2	1	2	3	1	2	2
Student 12	3	3	1	3	1	3	2	1	1	3	1	1	2	1	2	2	1	2	1	2
Student 13	3	3	1	1	4	1	3	3	1	3	2	2	2	2	3	2	3	1	2	2
Student 14	3	3	1	1	2	1	2	1	1	3	2	2	1	1	1	3	3	1	2	2
Student 15	3	1	3	1	4	1	3	3	1	3	2	1	1	2	3	2	1	1	2	1
Student 16	2	1	2	2	4	2	3	2	2	3	2	2	2	1	2	3	1	2	2	2
Student 17	3	1	1	1	4	1	3	3	1	3	2	2	2	2	2	2	3	1	2	2
Student 18	1	3	3	1	4	1	2	1	1	3	2	1	2	2	1	1	3	1	2	2

Objects

observations (18 students multiplied by 20 items). Here, the students are ordered in some type of pre-established order from top to bottom, either alphabetically, or by student number if the teacher wishes to keep the results anonymous. The items are ordered in the order in which they appear on the test. The answer key is provided in the second row along with person[1] responses to each item. In this example, the data are coded to where choice A = 1, choice B = 2, choice C = 3, and choice D = 4. Coding the responses as numerical input is important, as the analyses described in the chapter will be empirical in nature.

Once the observations are compiled into a data matrix, the next step is to convert the data matrix to a right/wrong matrix (see Table 8.2). For most multiple-choice tests, there is one correct answer and all other response options are incorrect. In these instances, every observation is either correct or incorrect. When the observations result in either a correct or incorrect response, the test responses are considered to be **dichotomous**. The right/wrong matrix is a representation of the dichotomous responses, coded as either 0 = incorrect (i.e., "wrong") or 1 = correct ("right"). The right/wrong matrix will form the foundation for much of the remaining data analysis processes.

Within the right/wrong matrix, the students can be ordered from highest ability to lowest ability based upon the *person sum score* (the total of correct answers for each person). Additionally, the items can be ordered from the least difficult to the most difficult based upon the *item sum score* (the total of correct answers for each item) (see Table 8.3). In creating these orderings, an interesting pattern emerges. If a diagonal line were to be drawn from the top right part of the matrix down to the bottom left part of the matrix, we would see that above the line, more 1s would emerge, particularly as the observations approach the top left part of the matrix (closest to the observation represented by the interaction between the highest ability student and least difficult item – Student 4 and Item 19) (see Figure 8.2). This indicates that the higher the person ability, the more likely the person is to respond correctly to a less difficult item. Oppositely, below the line, more 0s emerge, particularly as the observations approach the bottom right part of the matrix (closest to the observation represented by the interaction between the lowest ability student and most difficult item – Student 1 and Item 15. This indicates that the lower the person ability, the more likely the person is to respond incorrectly to a more difficult item. The closer that the observations approach the diagonal line, the more inconsistencies are observed, indicating more randomness to the response patterns.

The visual elements in the right/wrong matrix with the ordering of items and persons as described above provide more apparent insights into some inconsistencies in the response patterns. From an item perspective,

Table 8.2 Right/wrong matrix consisting of 360 dichotomously scored observations

Agents

	I01	I02	I03	I04	I05	I06	I07	I08	I09	I10	I11	I12	I13	I14	I15	I16	I17	I18	I19	I20
Student 1	0	0	0	0	1	0	0	0	0	1	1	0	0	0	1	1	0	1	0	0
Student 2	1	1	0	0	0	1	0	0	1	0	1	1	1	1	0	0	1	1	1	1
Student 3	0	0	0	0	0	0	1	0	1	0	0	1	1	1	0	0	0	1	1	1
Student 4	1	1	1	1	1	1	1	1	1	1	1	1	1	1	0	1	1	1	1	1
Student 5	1	1	1	1	1	1	0	1	1	1	1	0	1	1	0	1	1	1	1	1
Student 6	0	0	0	1	0	1	0	1	1	1	1	0	0	0	1	1	0	1	0	1
Student 7	0	0	0	1	0	0	0	1	0	0	0	0	1	1	0	0	0	0	1	1
Student 8	0	0	0	0	0	0	0	0	1	0	1	0	1	1	0	1	0	1	1	0
Student 9	0	0	1	1	1	1	1	0	1	1	1	1	0	1	0	0	0	1	1	1
Student 10	1	1	0	1	0	1	1	1	1	1	0	1	0	1	0	1	0	1	1	1
Student 11	1	1	1	1	1	0	0	0	1	1	0	1	1	0	0	1	1	1	1	1
Student 12	0	0	1	0	0	0	0	0	1	1	1	1	0	0	0	0	0	0	0	1
Student 13	1	0	1	1	1	1	0	1	1	1	1	0	1	1	0	1	0	1	1	1
Student 14	1	0	1	1	0	1	1	0	1	1	1	1	1	0	0	0	0	1	1	1
Student 15	1	1	0	1	1	0	1	1	0	1	1	1	0	1	0	1	1	1	1	1
Student 16	0	1	0	0	1	1	1	0	0	1	1	0	1	0	0	1	1	0	1	0
Student 17	1	1	1	1	1	1	0	1	1	1	1	0	0	1	0	1	0	1	1	1
Student 18	0	0	0	1	1	1	0	0	1	1	1	1	1	1	0	0	0	1	1	1

Objects

Table 8.3 Right/wrong matrix with ordering of students from high ability to low ability and ordering of items from least difficult to most difficult

Objects	Agents																				Person Sum Score
	I19	I20	I18	I10	I11	I09	I14	I04	I06	I13	I16	I01	I05	I02	I03	I08	I12	I07	I17	I15	
Student 4	1	1	1	1	1	1	1	1	1	1	1	1	1	1	1	1	1	1	1	0	19
Student 15	1	1	1	1	1	1	1	1	1	1	1	1	1	1	0	1	1	1	1	0	18
Student 11	1	1	1	0	1	1	1	1	1	1	1	1	1	1	1	0	1	1	0	0	16
Student 17	1	1	1	1	1	1	1	1	1	0	1	1	1	1	1	1	0	1	0	0	16
Student 13	1	1	1	1	1	1	1	1	1	0	1	1	1	0	1	1	1	0	0	1	16
Student 5	1	1	1	1	1	1	1	1	1	0	1	1	1	1	1	0	0	0	0	0	15
Student 10	1	1	1	1	1	1	1	1	1	1	0	1	1	1	1	0	0	0	0	0	13
Student 9	1	1	1	1	1	1	1	1	1	0	1	0	0	0	1	1	0	0	0	0	13
Student 6	1	1	1	1	1	1	0	1	1	1	1	0	0	0	0	1	1	0	0	1	12
Student 18	1	1	1	1	1	1	1	1	1	1	0	0	1	0	0	0	1	0	0	0	12
Student 14	1	1	1	1	1	1	0	1	1	1	0	1	0	0	1	0	0	0	0	0	11
Student 2	1	1	0	0	0	0	1	0	1	1	0	1	1	1	0	0	1	1	1	0	10
Student 16	1	0	0	1	1	0	0	0	0	1	0	0	1	0	0	0	0	1	1	1	9
Student 3	1	1	1	0	1	1	1	0	0	1	0	0	0	0	0	0	1	0	0	0	8
Student 8	1	1	1	0	1	1	1	0	0	0	1	0	0	0	0	0	0	0	0	0	7
Student 12	1	1	0	0	0	0	0	0	0	0	1	1	0	0	1	1	1	0	0	0	7
Student 7	1	1	1	0	0	1	1	1	0	1	0	0	0	0	0	1	0	0	0	0	6
Student 1	0	0	1	1	1	0	0	0	0	0	1	0	1	0	0	0	0	0	0	0	5
Item Sum Score	17	16	14	14	14	13	13	12	12	11	11	10	10	8	8	8	8	7	4	3	

Figure 8.2 Recognizing abnormalities in response patterns in the context of item- and person-ordering

Agents / Objects

	119	120	118	110	111	109	114	104	106	113	116	101	105	102	103	108	112	107	117	115	Person Sum Score
Student 4	1	1	1	1	1	1	1	1	1	1	1	1	1	1	1	1	1	1	1	0	19
Student 15	1	1	1	1	1	1	1	1	1	1	1	1	1	1	0	1	1	1	1	0	18
Student 11	1	1	1	1	0	1	1	1	1	1	1	1	1	1	1	1	1	0	0	0	16
Student 17	1	1	1	1	1	1	1	1	1	1	1	1	1	0	1	1	1	0	0	0	16
Student 13	1	1	1	1	1	1	1	1	1	0	1	1	1	1	0	1	1	1	0	0	16
Student 5	1	1	1	1	1	1	1	0	1	0	1	1	1	0	1	1	1	1	0	0	15
Student 10	1	1	1	1	1	1	1	1	1	1	1	0	1	1	0	0	0	0	0	0	13
Student 9	1	1	1	1	1	1	1	1	1	0	0	1	1	0	1	0	1	0	0	0	13
Student 6	1	1	1	1	1	1	1	1	1	1	1	1	0	0	0	0	0	0	0	0	12
Student 18	1	1	1	1	1	1	1	1	1	1	1	0	1	0	0	0	0	0	0	0	12
Student 14	1	1	1	1	1	1	1	1	1	1	1	0	0	0	0	0	0	0	0	0	11
Student 2	1	1	1	1	1	1	1	1	1	1	0	0	0	0	0	0	0	0	0	0	10
Student 16	1	0	1	1	1	1	1	1	1	1	0	0	0	0	0	0	0	0	0	0	9
Student 3	1	1	1	1	1	1	1	1	0	0	0	0	0	0	0	0	0	0	0	0	8
Student 8	1	1	1	1	1	1	1	0	0	0	0	0	0	0	0	0	0	0	0	0	7
Student 12	1	1	1	1	1	1	1	0	0	0	0	0	0	0	0	0	0	0	0	0	7
Student 7	1	1	1	1	1	1	0	0	0	0	0	0	0	0	0	0	0	0	0	0	6
Student 1	0	1	1	1	1	1	0	0	0	0	0	0	0	0	0	0	0	0	0	0	5
Item Sum Score	17	16	14	14	14	13	13	12	12	11	11	10	10	8	8	8	8	7	4	3	

we can look down the columns for areas where unexpected responses occur. Some examples include:

- *Item 13*: There is a string of correct responses for Students 14, 2, 16, and 3 where we would expect incorrect answers and a string of incorrect responses for Students 17, 13, and 5 where we would expect correct responses.
- *Item 12*: Students 18, 2, 3, and 12 answered correctly when we would expect them to answer incorrectly.
- *Item 14*: Students 3, 8, and 7 answered correctly when we would expect them to answer incorrectly.

The unexpected patterns in the item behavior provide an initial, qualitative awareness into potentially problematic items on the test from a class perspective.

From a person perspective, we can look across the rows for areas where unexpected responses occur. Some examples include:

- Student 11: Answered Item 11 incorrectly when it was expected to be answered correctly.
- Student 2: Answered some items incorrectly that were expected to be correct (Items 20, 18) and answered several items correctly that were expected to be incorrect (Items 1, 2, 12, 17).
- Student 16: Answered several items incorrectly that were expected to be correct (Items 18, 10, and 9) and answered several items correctly that were expected to be incorrect (Items 6, 13, 1, 2, 12, and 17).

The unexpected patterns in person behavior provide an initial, qualitative awareness into errors in the test taking procedure, guessing, or an atypical understanding/interpretation of instructional content from an individual student perspective.

Empirical Investigations Into Item and Person Functioning

The remainder of the chapter provides methods for empirically investigating item-centered and person-centered data. Item-centered data, or **item functioning**, play an important role in diagnosing and evaluating class-centered behaviors with their engagement with the test items through the evaluation of item response patterns. Person-centered data, or **person functioning**, play an important role in diagnosing and evaluating individual student-centered behaviors with their engagement with the test items through the evaluation of person response patterns.

Item Difficulty Indices

Item difficulty indices are important for exploring the proportion of students who answered an item correctly and incorrectly. Item difficulty is represented as a *p*-value (proportion value) and is calculated as follows:

$$P_i = \frac{R_i}{T_i},$$

where p_i = difficulty of item *i*,
   R_i = the sum of students who responded correctly to item *i*, and
   T_i = the total number of students who responded to item *i*.

From our example, if we were to calculate the item difficulty for Item 10, we see from Table 8.3 that a total of 14 students out of 20 answered the item correctly. Therefore, p_{i10} would be calculated as follows:

$$P_{i10} = \frac{14}{20} = 0.70.$$

The item difficulty calculations for all 20 items can be found in Table 8.4.
   The resulting values for item difficulty are a decimal ranging from 0.00 to 1.00. The closer the value approaches to 0.00, the more difficult the item is. The closer the value approaches to 1.00, the less difficult the item is. The decimal can also be interpreted as a percentage correct. In the case of Item 10, 0.70 (70%) of the students answered the item correctly. From a strict item analysis perspective,[2] item difficulty values can be interpreted as follows:

- *Easy item*: 0.75–1.00 (75%–100% of students answered the item correctly)
- *Average-difficulty item*: 0.25–0.75 (25%–75% of the students answered the item correctly)
- *Difficult item*: 0.00–0.25 (0%–25% of the students answered the item correctly)

According to Lord (1952), the ideal item difficulty in terms of discrimination potential for a five-response multiple-choice item is 0.70, the ideal item difficulty for a four-response multiple-choice item is 0.74, the ideal item difficulty for a three-response multiple-choice item is 0.77, and the ideal item difficulty for a true/false item or a two-response multiple-choice item is 0.85.

Person Ability Indices

Person ability indices are important for exploring the proportion of items that were answered correctly or incorrectly by an individual student. Person ability indices can be thought of conceptually and mathematically in

Table 8.4 Calculation of item difficulty for all 20 items

		Agents																			
		I19	I20	I18	I10	I11	I09	I14	I04	I06	I13	I16	I01	I05	I02	I03	I08	I12	I07	I17	I15
Objects	Student 4	1	1	1	1	1	1	1	1	1	1	1	1	1	1	1	1	1	1	1	0
	Student 15	1	1	1	1	1	1	1	1	1	1	1	1	1	1	0	1	1	1	1	0
	Student 11	1	1	1	1	0	1	1	1	1	1	1	1	1	1	1	0	1	1	0	0
	...	1	1	0	0	0	0	1	1	0	1	0	0	0	0	0	1	0	0	0	0
	Student 1	0	0	1	1	1	0	0	0	0	0	1	0	1	0	0	0	0	0	0	0
	Item Sum Score	17	16	14	14	14	13	13	12	12	11	11	10	10	8	8	8	8	7	4	3
	p_i	0.94	0.89	0.78	0.78	0.78	0.72	0.72	0.67	0.67	0.61	0.61	0.56	0.56	0.44	0.44	0.44	0.44	0.39	0.22	0.17

the same manner as item difficulty, only from a person-centered perspective. Person ability is also represented as a p-value (proportion value) and is calculated as follows:

$$P_p = \frac{R_p}{T_p},$$

where p_p = ability of person p,
R_p = the sum of the items that person p responded correctly to, and
T_p = the total number of items that person p responded to.

From the example, if we were to calculate the person ability for Student 17, we see from Table 8.3 that Student 17 answered a total of 16 out of the 20 items correctly. Therefore, $pp17$ would be calculated as follows:

$$P_{p17} = \frac{16}{20} = 0.80.$$

The person ability calculations for all 18 students can be found in Table 8.5.

Table 8.5 Calculation of person ability for all 18 students

		Agents					Person Sum Score	p_p
		I19	*I20*	*I18*	...	*I15*		
	Student 4	1	1	1	...	0	19	0.90
	Student 15	1	1	1	...	0	18	0.86
	Student 11	1	1	1	...	0	16	0.76
	Student 17	1	1	1	...	0	16	0.76
	Student 13	1	1	1	...	1	16	0.76
	Student 5	1	1	1	...	0	15	0.71
	Student 10	1	1	1	...	0	13	0.62
Objects	Student 9	1	1	1	...	0	13	0.62
	Student 6	1	1	1	...	1	12	0.57
	Student 18	1	1	1	...	0	12	0.57
	Student 14	1	1	1	...	0	11	0.52
	Student 2	1	1	0	...	0	10	0.48
	Student 16	1	0	0	...	1	9	0.43
	Student 3	1	1	1	...	0	8	0.38
	Student 8	1	1	1	...	0	7	0.33
	Student 12	1	1	0	...	0	7	0.33
	Student 7	1	1	0	...	0	6	0.29
	Student 1	0	0	1	...	0	5	0.24
	Item Sum Score	17	16	14	...	3		

Similarly to the interpretation of item difficulty values, person ability values result in a decimal ranging from 0.00 to 1.00. The closer the value approaches to 0.00, the lower-ability the person is. The closer the value approaches to 1.00, the higher-ability the person is. The decimal can also be interpreted as a percentage correct. In the case of Student 17, 0.80 (80%) of the items were answered correctly. From a strict person analysis perspective, person ability values can be interpreted as follows:

- *High-ability person*: 0.75–1.00 (75%–100% of items were answered correctly)
- *Average-ability person*: 0.25–0.75 (25%–75% of items were answered correctly)
- *Low-ability person*: 0.00–0.25 (0%–25% of items were answered correctly)

Item difficulty and person ability indices are proportion correct values that can be used to indicate a rank ordering of items (from least difficult to most difficult) and a rank ordering of persons (from highest-ability to lowest-ability). The problem with using only these indices, however, is that they do not provide any type of empirical quality indicator. According to Table 8.4, Items 18, 10, and 11 each have an item sum score of 14 with a *p*-value of 0.78. However, Table 8.3 indicates a different pattern of responses to each of the items. Therefore, although the *p*-values are the same, the quality of the item response patterns is different. Similarly, according to Table 8.5, Students 11, 17, and 17 each have a sum score of 16 with a *p*-value of 0.76. However, Table 8.3 indicates a different pattern of responses to each of the persons. Therefore, although the *p*-values are the same, the quality of the student response patterns is different. In order to empirically investigate the differences in quality of response patterns for both items and persons, item- and person-discrimination indices can be used.

Item-Discrimination Indices

Item-discrimination indices are important for empirically exploring the quality of the response patterns of the items. Conceptually, item-discrimination can be thought of as a value that represents the frequency with which items are responded to correctly by varying groups of ability levels of students, such as comparing high-ability student response patterns to low-ability response patterns, for example. Item discrimination is represented by a *D*-value (discrimination value) and is calculated as follows:

$$D_i = p_{i\_high} - p_{i\_low},$$

where D_i = discrimination of item i,
p_{i_high} = item difficulty index of the high-ability group, and
p_{i_low} = item difficulty index of the low-ability group.

In order to arrive at the calculation of D_i, there are some considerations to be made and steps to go through:

1. Start by creating a right/wrong matrix, ensuring that the persons are ordered from highest-ability to lowest-ability.
2. Divide the students evenly into a high-ability group and low-ability group. Some have suggested that the groups be divided into an upper 27% and a lower 27% (Kelley, 1939). This, however, assumes there is a large enough sample size. For the purpose of classroom music assessments, it is suggested to include all students by dividing the group into an equally divided upper 50% and lower 50%. If there is an uneven grouping of students, remove the middle-most student.
3. Calculate p_{i_high} (the item difficulty index for the high-ability group).
   a. Sum the total correct answers for the students in the high-ability group.
   b. Calculate the number of total students in the high-ability group.
   c. Divide the sum of the total correct answers for the students in the high-ability group by the total number of students in the high-ability group.
4. Calculate p_{i_low} (the item difficulty index for the low-ability group).
   a. Sum the total correct answers for the students in the low-ability group.
   b. Calculate the number of total students in the low-ability group.
   c. Divide the sum of the total correct answers for the students in the low-ability group by the total number of students in the low-ability group.
5. Calculate D_i (the item discrimination index).
   a. Subtract the item difficulty index of the low-ability group (p_{i_low}) from the item difficulty index of the high-ability group (p_{i_high}).

As an example, let us calculate the item discrimination index for Item 4. If we evaluate the ordered right/wrong matrix displayed in Table 8.6, we see that the students are evenly split (50/50) into a high-ability group and a low-ability group, consisting of nine students each. The grey shading indicates the high-ability group. In order to calculate the item difficulty index for the high-ability group (p_{i_high}), divide the sum of the total correct answers for the students in the high-ability group (nine) by the total number of students in the high-ability group (nine). The item difficulty index for the high-ability group is equal to 1.00. Substantively, 100% of the students in the high-ability group answered Item 4 correctly. In order to calculate the item difficulty index for the low-ability group (p_{i_low}), divide the sum of the total correct answers for the students in the low-ability group (three) by the total number of students in the low-ability group (nine). The item difficulty index for the low-ability group is equal to 0.33. Substantively, 33% of the students in the low-ability group answered Item 4 correctly. To calculate the item discrimination index for Item 4 (D_{i4}), subtract the item difficulty index of the low-ability group (p_{i_low} = 0.33) from the item difficulty index of the high-ability group (p_{i_high} = 1.00). The item discrimination index for Item 4 (D_{i4}) is equal to 0.67.

The item discrimination indices for each of the 20 items are found in Table 8.6. In evaluating these indices, values range from –1.00 to 1.00. There are two pieces of information that can be gleaned from their values: (a) directionality and (b) range. Positively discriminating items (values greater than 0.00) indicate that the high-ability group more often answers the item correctly than the lower-ability group (high-ability group scores > lower-ability group scores). Negatively discriminating items (values less than 0.00) indicate that the low-ability group more often answers the item correctly than the high-ability group (high-ability group scores < low-ability group scores). Non-discriminating items (values equal or close to 0.00) indicate that there is no substantial difference between the high-ability group score and low-ability group score on the item (high-ability group scores = low-ability group scores). From a data analysis perspective, music teachers would hope to find their items to be positively discriminating, indicating that the students in the high-ability group are more often answering the questions correctly than the students in the low-ability group.

The range of the discrimination index quantifies the quality of the relationship between class ability and answering the item correctly. The values can be interpreted as follows:

- *Very good item*: 0.40–1.00 (use; class responses are trustworthy).
- *Reasonably good item*: 0.30–0.39 (consider revising item; consider investigating class responses).
- *Fairly good item*: 0.11–0.29 (revise item; definitely investigate class responses).
- *Poor item*: 0.00–0.10 (do not use item; class responses are not trustworthy).

Note that the relationship between the interpretative categories and number ranges for item discrimination is different than the interpretative categories and number ranges for item difficulty. In practice, item discrimination indices rarely exceed 0.50 due to various distributions in the relationships between item performance and total test scores.

Negatively discriminating items or items with low discrimination values provide evidence that, from a class perspective, something is wrong with either the testing context (e.g., mistake in the answer collection

Table 8.6 Calculation of item discrimination indices

		Agents																			
		I19	I20	I18	I10	I11	I09	I14	I04	I06	I13	I16	I01	I05	I02	I03	I08	I12	I07	I17	I15
Objects	Student 4	1	1	1	1	1	1	1	1	1	1	1	1	1	1	1	1	1	1	1	0
	Student 15	1	1	1	1	1	1	1	1	1	1	1	1	1	1	0	1	1	1	1	0
	Student 11	1	1	1	1	0	1	1	1	1	1	1	1	1	1	1	0	0	1	0	0
	Student 17	1	1	1	1	1	1	1	1	1	0	1	1	1	0	1	1	1	1	0	0
	Student 13	1	1	1	1	1	1	1	1	1	0	1	1	1	1	1	1	1	1	0	1
	Student 5	1	1	1	1	1	1	1	1	1	0	0	0	1	0	0	1	0	0	0	0
	Student 10	1	1	1	1	1	1	1	1	1	1	1	1	0	1	1	1	1	1	0	0
	Student 9	1	1	1	1	1	1	1	1	1	0	1	0	1	0	1	1	0	0	0	0
	Student 6	1	1	1	1	1	1	0	1	1	1	1	1	0	0	0	1	0	0	0	1
	Student 18	1	1	1	1	1	1	1	1	1	1	0	0	1	0	0	0	1	0	0	0
	Student 14	1	1	1	1	1	1	0	1	1	1	0	1	0	0	1	0	0	0	0	0
	Student 2	1	1	0	0	1	0	1	0	1	1	0	1	1	1	0	0	1	0	0	0
	Student 16	1	0	0	1	1	0	0	0	0	1	0	0	1	1	0	0	0	0	1	1
	Student 3	1	1	1	0	0	1	1	1	0	1	0	0	0	0	0	0	0	1	0	0
	Student 8	1	1	1	0	1	1	1	0	0	0	1	0	0	0	0	0	0	0	0	0
	Student 12	1	1	0	1	0	0	0	0	0	0	1	1	0	1	1	0	1	0	0	0
	Student 7	1	1	0	0	0	0	1	0	0	1	0	0	0	0	0	0	0	0	0	0
	Student 1	0	0	1	1	1	0	0	0	0	0	1	0	0	0	0	0	0	0	1	0
	Item Sum Score	17	16	14	14	14	13	13	12	12	11	11	10	10	8	8	8	8	7	4	3

p_i	0.94	0.89	0.78	0.78	0.72	0.72	0.67	0.67	0.61	0.61	0.56	0.56	0.44	0.44	0.44	0.39	0.22	0.17
# correct high	9	9	9	9	8	9	9	9	8	8	7	7	6	7	4	5	2	2
p_{i_high}	1.00	1.00	1.00	1.00	0.89	1.00	1.00	0.89	0.78	0.89	0.78	0.67	0.67	0.78	0.44	0.56	0.22	0.22
# correct low	8	7	5	6	4	5	3	3	6	3	3	2	2	1	4	2	2	1
p_{i_low}	0.89	0.78	0.56	0.67	0.44	0.56	0.33	0.33	0.67	0.33	0.33	0.22	0.22	0.11	0.44	0.22	0.22	0.11
D_i	0.11	0.22	0.44	0.44	0.22	0.56	0.67	0.67	-0.11	0.56	0.44	0.44	0.44	0.67	0.00	0.33	0.00	0.11

Note. Grey shading indicates high-ability group.

process), the item (e.g., the writing style, misleading answers, wrong information), the instructional delivery underscoring the content of the item (e.g., content was never covered, did not convey answer), or the students' understanding of the content knowledge (e.g., class confusion about a topic, guessing). Therefore, these items should be removed from the testing context when considering the evaluation of student learning outcomes. Furthermore, engagement with the class about the testing context and class knowledge of the content is encouraged.

Person-Discrimination Indices

Person-discrimination indices are important for empirically exploring the quality of the response patterns of the individual students. Conceptually, person-discrimination can be thought of as a value that represents the frequency with which students responded correctly to items by varying groups of difficulty levels of items, such as comparing more difficult item response patterns to less difficult item response patterns, for example. Similar to item-discrimination, person-discrimination is represented by a D-value (discrimination value) and is calculated as follows:

$$D_p = p_{p\_easy} - p_{p\_difficult}$$

where D_p = discrimination of person i,
p_{p_easy} = person ability index of the less-difficult item group, and
$p_{p\_difficult}$ = person ability index of the more-difficult item group.

In order to arrive at the calculation of D_p, there are some considerations to be made and steps to go through:

1. Start by creating a right/wrong matrix, ensuring that the items are ordered from least difficult to most difficult.
2. Divide the items evenly into a more-difficult group and less-difficult group. Divide the groups into an equal 50/50 split (50% more-difficult and 50% less-difficult). If there is an uneven grouping of items, remove the middle-most item.
3. Calculate $p_{p\_less\_difficult}$ (the person ability index for the less-difficult item group).

    a. Sum the total correct answers for the items in the less-difficult item group.
    b. Calculate the number of total items in the less-difficult item group.
    c. Divide the sum of the total correct answers for the items in the less-difficult item group by the total number of items in the less-difficult item group.

4. Calculate $p_{p\_more\_difficult}$ (the person ability index for the more-difficult item group).

    a. Sum the total correct answers for the items in the more-difficult item group.

    b. Calculate the number of total items in the more-difficult item group.

    c. Divide the sum of the total correct answers for the items in the more-difficult item group by the total number of items in the more-difficult item group.

5. Calculate D_p (the person ability index).

    a. Subtract the person ability index of the more-difficult item group ($p_{p\_more\_difficult}$) from the person ability index of the less-difficult item group ($p_{p\_less\_difficult}$).

As an example, let us calculate the person ability index for Student 6. If we evaluate the ordered right/wrong matrix displayed in Table 8.7, we see that the items are evenly split (50/50) into a more-difficult item group and a less-difficult item group, consisting of ten items each. The grey shading indicates the less-difficult item group. In order to calculate the person ability index for the less-difficult item group ($p_{p\_less\_difficult}$), divide the sum of the total correct answers for the items in the less-difficult item group (nine) by the total number of items in the less-difficult item group (ten). The person ability index for the less-difficult item group is equal to 0.90. Substantively, Student 6 answered 90% of the items in the less-difficult item group correctly. In order to calculate the person ability index for the more-difficult item group ($p_{p\_more\_difficult}$), divide the sum of the total correct answers for the items in the more-difficult item group (three) by the total number of items in the more-difficult item group (ten). The person ability index for the more-difficult item group is equal to 0.30. Substantively, Student 6 answered 30% of the items in the difficult item group correctly. To calculate the person ability index for Student 6 (D_{s6}), subtract the person ability index of the more-difficult item group ($p_{p\_more\_difficult} = 0.30$) from the person ability index of the less-difficult item group ($p_{p\_less\_difficult} = 0.90$). The item discrimination index for student 6 (D_{p6}) is equal to 0.60.

The person ability indices for each of the 18 students are found in Table 8.7.

Similar to the item discrimination indices, values range from −1.00 to 1.00. The positively discriminating persons (values greater than 0.00) indicate that the less-difficult item grouping was more often answered correctly than the more-difficult item grouping (more-difficult item group scores > less-difficult item group scores). Negatively discriminating persons (values less than 0.00) indicate that the more-difficult item grouping was more often answered correctly than the less-difficult item grouping (less-difficult item group scores < more-difficult item group scores).

Table 8.7 Calculation of person discrimination indices

	Agents																				Person p_v Sum Score		# correct less-dif	p_{i_easy}	# correct more-dif	p_{i_dif}	D_v
	I19	I20	I18	I10	I11	I09	I14	I04	I06	I13	I16	I01	I05	I02	I03	I08	I12	I07	I17	I15							
S4	1	1	1	1	1	1	1	1	1	1	1	1	1	1	1	1	1	1	1	0	19	0.90	10	1.00	9	0.90	0.10
S15	1	1	1	1	1	1	1	1	1	1	1	1	1	1	1	0	1	1	1	0	18	0.86	10	1.00	8	0.80	0.20
S11	1	1	1	0	1	1	1	1	1	1	1	1	1	1	0	1	1	0	1	0	16	0.76	9	0.90	7	0.70	0.20
S17	1	1	1	1	1	1	1	1	1	1	1	1	1	1	1	0	1	0	0	0	16	0.76	9	0.90	7	0.70	0.20
S13	1	1	1	1	1	1	1	1	1	1	1	1	1	1	1	0	0	0	1	0	16	0.76	9	0.90	7	0.70	0.20
S5	1	1	1	1	1	1	1	1	1	1	1	1	1	1	1	0	0	0	0	0	15	0.71	9	0.90	6	0.60	0.30
S10	1	1	1	1	1	1	1	1	1	1	0	0	1	0	0	0	1	0	0	0	13	0.62	10	1.00	3	0.30	0.70
S9	1	1	1	1	1	1	1	1	1	1	1	0	0	1	0	1	0	0	0	0	13	0.62	9	0.90	4	0.40	0.50
S6	1	1	1	1	1	1	1	0	1	1	1	0	1	0	0	0	1	0	0	0	12	0.57	9	0.90	3	0.30	0.60
S18	1	1	1	1	1	1	1	1	1	1	0	0	1	0	1	0	1	0	0	0	12	0.57	10	1.00	2	0.20	0.80
S14	1	1	1	1	1	0	1	0	1	1	0	1	0	0	1	0	0	0	0	0	11	0.52	9	0.90	2	0.20	0.70
S2	1	0	0	1	0	0	0	1	1	1	1	1	1	1	0	0	1	1	1	1	10	0.48	6	0.60	4	0.40	0.20
S16	1	0	1	1	0	1	0	0	0	1	0	0	1	1	0	0	0	1	1	0	9	0.43	4	0.40	5	0.50	-0.10
S3	1	1	1	0	1	1	0	0	0	1	0	0	0	0	0	0	1	0	0	0	8	0.38	6	0.60	2	0.20	0.40
S8	1	1	0	1	1	1	1	0	0	0	1	0	0	0	0	0	0	0	0	0	7	0.33	6	0.60	1	0.10	0.50
S12	1	1	1	0	0	0	0	0	0	1	1	1	0	0	1	1	1	1	0	0	7	0.33	3	0.30	4	0.40	-0.10
S7	1	1	1	0	0	0	1	1	0	0	0	0	0	0	0	1	0	0	0	0	6	0.29	5	0.50	1	0.10	0.40
S1	0	0	0	1	0	0	0	0	0	0	1	0	1	0	0	0	0	0	0	0	5	0.24	3	0.30	2	0.20	0.10

Objects

Non-discriminating items (values equal or close to 0.00) indicate that there is no substantial difference between the less-difficult item group scores and more-difficult item group scores by the student (less-difficult item scores = more-difficult item scores). From a data analysis perspective, music teachers would hope to find their students to be positively discriminating, indicating that the student is answering the less-difficult items correctly more frequently than the more-difficult items.

The range of the discrimination quantifies the quality of the relationship between item difficulty and individual student ability. The values can be interpreted as follows:

- *Good-quality responses*: 0.40–1.00 (use student outcome data; patterns in student responses are acceptable).
- *Reasonable-quality responses*: 0.30–0.39 (use student outcome data with some caution; consider investigating student responses; patterns in student responses are somewhat acceptable).
- *Fair-quality responses*: 0.11–0.29 (consider not using student outcome data; investigate student responses; patterns in student responses are somewhat unacceptable).
- *Poor-quality responses*: 0.00–0.10 (do not use student outcome data; definitely investigate student responses; student responses are unacceptable).

The values can be interpreted in the same manner as item discrimination indices. However, these indices are now student-centered (as opposed to class-centered) and provide a mechanism to investigate individual students and the adequacy of their learning. Negatively discriminating students or students with low discrimination values provide evidence that, from a student perspective, something is wrong with either the testing context (e.g., mistakes in the answer keying process, did not understand directions, skipped/did not answer items), the student himself or herself (e.g., did not engage the test, sick, distracted), the instructional delivery underscoring the content (e.g., missed instruction, did not study material covered), or the student's understanding of the content knowledge (e.g., individual student confusion about a topic, guessing). Therefore, these students should be removed from the testing context when considering the quality of the evaluation of student learning outcomes. Furthermore, engagement/intervention with the individual student or students' parents about the testing context and acquisition/understanding of instructional content is encouraged.

Distractor Analyses

In the event that the music educator finds item difficulty indices, person ability indices, item-discrimination indices, or person-discrimination indices that are problematic and warrant follow-up with either the class (for item-related abnormalities in the data) or individual students (for person-related abnormalities in the data), distractor analyses can be conducted as a means to further investigate more substantive issues pertaining to item and/or person response patterns.

Item Distractor Analyses

If we revisit the item difficulty (p_i) indices and item-discrimination (D_i) indices from Table 8.6, we can see that Item 13 is a suitable item for further investigation and possible class discussion. Item 13 demonstrated an item difficulty of 0.61 and an item-discrimination of –0.11. The item is considered average-difficulty; however, the discrimination index indicates that more lower-ability students answered the item correctly than high-ability students. If we revisit the original observations displayed in Table 8.1 and investigate the dichotomous responses of the high group and low group to Item 13 (Table 8.2), we can extrapolate the full details of the response patterns and display them in a table similar to the one reflected in Table 8.8. After evaluating the item distractor analysis for Item 13, we see that response option 3 and response option 4 were never selected. If we were to revise the item for future use, we may wish to eliminate both options 3 and 4 since all students clearly viewed them as inappropriate responses. The negative discrimination index indicates that more students from the low-ability group answered Item 13 correctly than students from the high-ability group. As we can see, 66.7% of the low-ability-group students answered the item correct compared to 55.6% of the students from the high-ability group. There is clearly something enticing in response option 2 for the students to respond to, as members of the low-ability group (33.3%) and high-ability group (44.4%) selected response option 2. Therefore, the teacher may wish to address why this occurred from a content perspective. If it is a problem with the item itself or the instructional delivery, the teacher should make adjustments to the item and/or instructional delivery for the next instructional/assessment cycle and then reevaluate the question after the completion of the next cycle's test. If it is a content-related concern, an open class discussion and instructional follow-up may be necessary to improve overall student understanding of the instructional content underscoring Item 13.

Person Distractor Analyses

If we revisit the person ability (p_p) indices and person-discrimination (D_p) indices from Table 8.7, we can see that Student 16 is a suitable person for further investigation and possible individual student conversation/intervention. Student 16 demonstrated a person ability of 0.43 and a person-discrimination of –0.10. Student 16 is considered an average-ability student; however, the discrimination index indicates that as member of the low-ability group, he or she answered more-difficult answers correctly and less-difficult items incorrectly than members of the high-ability group. If we revisit the original observations displayed in Table 8.1 and investigate

Table 8.8 Item distractor analysis for Item 13

	Response option 1 *		Response option 2		Response option 3		Response option 4	
	Frequency	%	Frequency	%	Frequency	%	Frequency	%
High Group	5	55.6%	4	44.4%	0	0.00%	0	0.00%
Low Group	6	66.7%	3	33.3%	0	0.00%	0	0.00%

Note. High-group students (in rank order) include 4, 15, 11, 17, 13, 5, 10, 9 and 6. Low-group students (in rank order) include Students 18, 14, 2, 16, 3, 8, 12, 7, and 1.
* indicates correct answer.

Table 8.9 Item distractor analysis for Item 13

Person Distractor Analysis for Student 16

			High Group		Low Group	
Item	p_i	Observation	% Correct	% Incorrect	% Correct	% Incorrect
Item 15	0.17	1	0.11	0.89	0.22	0.78
Item 17	0.22	1	0.22	0.78	0.22	0.78
Item 7	0.39	1	0.56	0.44	0.22	0.78
Item 2	0.44	1	0.67	0.33	0.22	0.78
Item 3	0.44	0	0.67	0.33	0.22	0.78
Item 8	0.44	0	0.67	0.33	0.22	0.78
Item 12	0.44	0	0.56	0.44	0.33	0.67
Item 1	0.56	0	0.78	0.22	0.33	0.67
Item 5	0.56	1	0.89	0.11	0.22	0.78
Item 13	0.61	1	0.56	0.44	0.67	0.33
Item 16	0.61	0	0.78	0.22	0.44	0.56
Item 4	0.67	0	1.00	0.00	0.33	0.67
Item 6	0.67	0	1.00	0.00	0.33	0.67
Item 9	0.72	0	1.00	0.00	0.44	0.56
Item 14	0.72	0	1.00	0.00	0.44	0.56
Item 10	0.78	1	1.00	0.00	0.56	0.44
Item 11	0.78	1	0.89	0.11	0.67	0.33
Item 18	0.78	0	1.00	0.00	0.56	0.44
Item 20	0.89	0	1.00	0.22	0.78	0.22
Item 19	0.94	1	1.00	0.00	0.89	0.11

the dichotomous responses of the less-difficult items and more- difficult items for Student 16 (Table 8.3), we can extrapolate the full details of the response patterns and display them in a table similar to the one reflected in Table 8.9. After evaluating the person distractor analysis for Student 16, we see the student answered the four most difficult items correctly (Items 15, 17, 7 and 2), which is completely unexpected. We also see that there is an interesting pattern of correct responses and incorrect responses as related to the ordering of items from more-difficult to less-difficult. In the context of an authentic assessment scenario, there may be any number of student-centered reasons for the results, such as implications for understanding of the content underlying the items, opportunity-to-learn considerations, attendance, or a unique interpretation of instructional content delivery. Table 8.9 provides new empirical insights into how this individual student demonstrates learning of the instructional material, and the results of the person-discrimination indices have brought needed attention to this student for possible intervention. In this instance, a one-on-one meeting with the student is encouraged in order to better understand their unique interpretation of the content and/or testing considerations that may have affected their performance on the test.

Summarizing Results

As Wright and Stone (1979) note, there are three important properties of any test (T): (a) test height (H), (b) test width (W), and (c) test length (L). Test height (H) refers to the average difficulty of the test items. Test width (W) refers to the ability range of the persons taking the test. Test length (L) refers to the number of items used in the test. According to Wright, this information can be extracted and reported as follows: T (H, W L).

In order to report the test height (H), we can calculate the average difficulty of the test items. If we calculate the average item difficulty (p_i) values across the p_i row in Table 8.6, we get a value of 0.59. Using the same item difficulty interpretations listed above, we can conclude that the test is of average difficulty. In order to report the test width (W), we can evaluate the range of person ability. According to Table 8.7, the range of person ability is from 0.24 to 0.90. Using the same person ability value interpretations listed above, we can conclude that the persons range from low-ability to high-ability, with an average of 0.56 (average-ability). More specifically, persons consisted of 1 low-ability student (Student 1), 12 average-ability students (Students 7, 12, 8, 3, 16, 2, 14, 18, 6, 9, 10, and 5), and 5 high-ability students (Students 13, 17, 11, 15, and 4). Using Wright's suggestion, the test-centered properties can be reported as:

Instrument Timbre Test (0.59, 0.24–0.90, 20).

This report includes all items and persons. If we exclude items with low or negative discrimination indices (Items 13, 12, 17; see Table 8.6) and persons with low or negative discrimination indices (Persons 4, 16, 12, 1), the test-centered properties can be reported as:

Instrument Timbre Test (0.62, 0.29–0.86, 17).

Validity, Reliability, and Fairness Follow-Up Considerations

We noted that there were some quality concerns with the patterns of responses related to some items and some persons. In these cases, the items and persons with unexpected response patterns are not necessarily a quality representation of the overall assessment context. Therefore, from a student-centered perspective, it is the music educator's ethical responsibility to consider whether there are any validity, reliability, or fairness concerns that are associated with these unexpected outcomes. It is suggested that the questions aligned to each of the validity, reliability, and fairness quality indicators described in Chapter 5 be revisited and considered as possible influencers for the outcomes of the unexpected response patterns observed in the testing outcomes.

A Note on Polytomous Items

The example outlined in this chapter was a multiple-choice test that resulted in dichotomous (correct/incorrect) responses. In many instances, particularly in the context of music performance assessments, rating scales or rubrics may be used to evaluate student performance. For these types of evaluation instruments, there may be more than two response categories associated with the criteria. As an example, a Likert-type rating scale may include four response categories such as *Strongly Disagree, Disagree, Agree*, and *Strongly Agree*. A rubric may include four response categories such as *Emerging, Approaching Standard, Meeting Standard*, and *Exceeding Standard*. In instances where response categories include more than two options, they are said to be **polytomous**. For polytomous items, item difficulty, person ability, item-discrimination, and person-discrimination indices are calculated in the same manner as dichotomous items (as described in this chapter). Fundamentally, each of these indices are calculated using proportions. For example:

Item difficulty is calculated as:

$$p_i = \frac{R_i}{T_i},$$

Person ability is calculated as:

$$p_p = \frac{R_p}{T_p},$$

Item-discrimination is calculated as:

$$D_i = \left(\frac{sum\, correct\, answers\, high - ability\, group}{total\, students\, high - ability\, group} \right) - \\ \left(\frac{sum\, correct\, answers\, low - ability\, group}{total\, students\, low - ability\, group} \right)$$

Person-discrimination is calculated as:

$$D_p = \left(\frac{sum\,correct\,answers\,less\,difficult\,item\,group}{total\,item\,less\,difficult\,group} \right) - \left(\frac{sum\,correct\,answers\,more\,difficult\,item\,group}{total\,item\,more\,difficult\,group} \right)$$

As a result, the calculations will hold true with more than two response options. However, there are three important requirements for this to work. First, all of the criteria must have the same response category structure. As an example, having one criterion with a response category structure of *Approaching Standard/Meeting Standard* and another criterion with a response category structure of *Approaching Standard/Meeting Standard/Exceeding Standard* will not work. Second, the response categories must be coded in the same, ascending order. As an example, if there are four categories for every criterion, the lowest category should be labeled 1, the second category should be labeled 2, the third category should be labeled 3, and the highest category should be labeled 4. Lastly, the same label should represent each response category across all criteria. As an example, if each criterion has the response category *Strongly Disagree, Disagree, Agree,* and *Strongly Agree, Strongly Disagree* will always be coded as a 1 for every criterion, *Disagree* will always be coded as a 2 for every criterion, *Agree* will always be coded as a 3 for every criterion, and *Strongly Agree* will always be coded as a 4 for every criterion. If there are four response categories, the total possible amount a student can score is 4 points.

Summary

It is important to clearly communicate to administrators and stakeholders the teaching and learning occurring in the music classroom with empirical data. Additionally, it is important to examine assessment data using empirical methods as a means to explore the quality of students' learning. There are four important indices that provide insights into the outcomes and quality of testing data: (a) item difficulty indices, (b) person ability indices, (c) item-discrimination indices, and (d) person-discrimination indices. Item difficulty is an important index for exploring the proportion of students who answered an item correctly and incorrectly. Person ability is an important index for exploring the proportion of items that were answered correctly or incorrectly by an individual student. Item-discrimination is an important index for empirically exploring the quality of the response patterns of the items. Person-discrimination is an important index for empirically exploring the quality of the response patterns of the individual students. In the case that there are abnormalities in the outcome data, item and person distractor analyses as well as the qualitative considerations for the validity, reliability, and fairness of student outcomes are important tools to inform future teaching and learning processes and improving future test uses from both a class-centered perspective and an individual student-centered perspective.

Activity Worksheet

	Item 01	Item 02	Item 03	Item 04	Item 05	Item 06	Item 07	Item 08	Item 09	Item 10
Student 01	1	1	0	1	1	0	1	1	1	1
Student 02	1	0	1	1	1	0	1	1	0	1
Student 03	1	0	1	1	1	0	1	1	0	0
Student 04	1	0	0	0	1	1	1	1	1	0
Student 05	1	1	0	1	0	1	0	1	0	0
Student 06	1	0	0	1	1	0	1	1	1	0
Student 07	1	1	1	0	1	0	1	0	0	0
Student 08	1	1	1	0	1	0	0	0	0	0
Student 09	1	1	0	0	0	0	0	1	0	0
Student 10	0	1	1	0	0	0	0	0	1	0

Above is a sample right/wrong matrix. A total of 100 observations were collected. The data are dichotomously scored and represent 10 students responding to 10 items. Complete the following:

1. Sum the person scores.
2. Sum the item scores.
3. Rearrange the right/wrong matrix by ordering the items from least difficult to most difficult and persons from highest-achieving to lowest-achieving.
4. Draw a diagonal line from the top right part of the matrix down to the bottom left part of the matrix.
5. Document any items and persons where unexpected responses are occurring.
6. Calculate an item difficulty index for each item.
7. Which items are considered easy? Which items are considered average-difficulty? Which items are considered difficult?
8. Calculate a person ability index for each person.
9. Which persons are considered high-ability? Which persons are considered average-ability? Which persons are considered low-ability?
10. Split the items into a 50% less-difficult group and 50% more-difficult group.
11. Calculate an item-discrimination index for each item.

12. Which items are considered very good items? Which items are considered reasonably good items? Which items are considered fairly good items? Which items are considered poor items?

13. Calculate a person-discrimination index for each person.

14. Which persons are considered to have provided good-quality responses? Which persons are considered to have provided reasonable-quality responses? Which persons are considered to have provided fair-quality responses? Which persons are considered to have provided poor-quality responses?

15. Choose one negatively discriminating item/poor item and construct an item distractor analysis table.

16. Choose one negatively discriminating person/poor-quality-response person and construct a person distractor analysis table.

17. Report the test height, test width, and test length including all items and persons.

18. Report the test height, test width, and test length after excluding the negatively discriminating item/poor items and the negatively discriminating person/poor-quality-response persons.

Notes

1. When evaluating testing data, the term *person* is used to reflect the group of students, or objects of measurement. When broadly discussing the syntax of the data, the term *person* will be used. When discussing the individual test performance or student in context of the classroom, the term *student* will be used.

2. When providing an interpretation of item *difficulty* or person *ability*, it is from a strict data analysis perspective, not necessary the teacher's interpretation of "difficulty" of an item or "ability" of a student in the context of teaching and learning/classroom expectations.

References

Hart, K. (2003). From an administrator's perspective: Practical survival skills for music educators. *Music Educators Journal*, 90(2), 41–45.

Kelley, T. L. (1939). The selection of upper and lower groups for the validation of test items. *Journal of Educational Psychology*, 30, 17–24.

Lord, F. M. (1952). The relationship of the reliability of multiple-choice test to the distribution of item difficulties. *Psychometrika*, 18, 181–194.

National Comprehensive Center for Teacher Quality. (2011). *Measuring teachers' contributions to student learning growth and non-tested grades and subjects*. Washington, DC: Educational Testing Service.

Wesolowski, B. C. (2014). Documenting student learning in music performance: A framework. *Music Educators Journal*, 101(1), 77–85.

Wesolowski, B. C. (2015). Tracking student achievement in music performance: Developing student learning objectives for growth model assessments. *Music Educators Journal*, 102(1), 39–47.

Wright, B. D., & Stone, M. H. (1979). *Best test design*. Chicago, IL: MESA Press.

9 Using Assessment for Program Improvement

Phillip Payne and Frederick Burrack

Chapter Overview

This chapter addresses using assessment to enhance program development. In program development, assessment data are collected to guide music teachers toward decisions regarding curriculum, structure, staffing, and student learning through a comprehensive program assessment plan. Upon completion of the chapter, music teachers will possess a deeper knowledge of the program assessment processes, will understand how to use program assessment for improvement, and will develop a program assessment plan using program-embedded assignments.

Learning Expectations for the Chapter

- Describe the usefulness of assessment as the foundation for program review and improvement.
- Create a variety of strategies to measure learning across a curriculum.
- Design and develop a program assessment plan focused on student learning.

Essential Questions for the Chapter

- How are assessments developed and integrated within a music program?
- How are assessment data used to inform decisions made for program improvement?
- What strategies exist that address creating and implementing assessment across the curriculum?

Introduction

A shared definition of learning in a music program is often difficult to articulate and equally challenging to advocate among relevant stakeholders regarding program vitality. Therefore, establishing a framework to help organize all these data should be a focus for faculty and program directors. The quality of music education is becoming a national priority. In 2015, the NafME revised and refined their Opportunity to Learn Standards (OtLS) that provide parameters and guidelines for defining basic and quality programs (National Association for Music Education, 2015). These documents provide an excellent framework for reviewing programs and organizing assessment-related data. Among the areas the OtLS address are (a) Curriculum and Scheduling, (b) Staffing, (c) Materials and Equipment, and (d) Facilities. Subsections in each of these areas include descriptors and indicators of basic and quality programs. These guidelines are intended to be used to support programs for continual development. A groundswell of interest by music teachers, educational administrators, and policy makers should develop into opportunities to assess what students gain from their studies in music and using this information to enhance the quality of instruction. A fundamental step is determining the extent to which students in our school have a fair and equal opportunity to learn music.

Learning Experience: Using the framework for the OtLS seen in the table below, write in the boxes what you believe are required for basic music programs. Identify the needs, what causes immediate impact, typical requests, and common funding sources in the areas of (a) Curriculum and Scheduling, (b) Staffing, (c) Materials and Equipment, and (d) Facilities. Then, compare your beliefs with those stated in the OtLS published on the NafME website.

National Association for Music Education	Identify Needs	Immediate Impact on Students	Long-term Resource Solution (Request)	Funding Source or Other Solution
Curriculum and Scheduling				
Staffing				
Materials and Equipment				
Facilities				

While the OtLS are helpful, they are primarily standards focused on needs to deliver quality instruction. Program assessment encompasses a much broader set of considerations beyond the four areas of the OtLS including student learning. The EDUCAUSE Learning Initiative (2019) identified ten *key issues* in teaching and learning of which six were assessment-related. These included establishing and supporting a culture of evidence to documenting learning growth, creating engaging learning activities aimed to meet program objectives, and being more effective in analyzing student learning to inform instructional practice. This is supportive of Campbell and Oblinger (2007), who identified more than a decade earlier that establishing and supporting a culture of evidence along with documenting learning growth are among the top issues in education. Documenting student learning and establishing a framework for making program improvements remain an important issue for educators at all levels and all disciplines. One way to address these issues is to integrate a variety of assessment measures throughout a curriculum with the aim to provide information to educationally and operationally improve the program. This chapter explores a process and rationale by which data on program maintenance measure effectiveness and how programs can use student-learning assessments to improve the quality and delivery of a music program.

Program Assessment

In the past, it was typical for teachers to remain disconnected from matters beyond classroom instruction; however, confirming the value and oversight of a music program in the school is as much the responsibility of music educators as it is of program directors and building administrators. Many music teachers have learned to accept their responsibility for the organization and administration of their school music program. An annual program review has become a vital part of **program assessment**. Annual **program review** includes (a) confirming and reviewing the program mission and **program learning goals**; (b) reviewing and updating curricular scope of content and instructional sequence; (c) confirming course learning expectations and assessment measures; (d) maintaining ongoing review of student learning achievement data; (e) detailed documentation of enrollment; (f) engagement with community; and (g) overall program achievements. The key to program review is to document evidence that represents the complex nature of music learning in the lives of your students and to identify ways to use that evidence to improve student and program performance.

Common Components of Program Review

Mission Statement

A **mission statement** is a critical step in establishing a solid and lasting program. Developing a mission statement that authentically reflects instructional activities and student learning in your music program requires thoughtful discussion among all music teachers in the school. Consensus while developing a well-structured mission statement results in cohesive curriculum and collaborative collegiality. A well-defined, clear mission statement should reveal the program's primary purpose and its organizational structure and is intended to guide all decisions within the program (Kokemuller, 2018). Focused vision leads to effective enrollment management, retention, instructional content, curriculum, staffing, and assessments.

Learning Experience: Write a mission statement for your future music program. Be comprehensive, but succinct, in your expectations of your program. Collaborating in pairs or groups, as if colleagues across a music program, may provide a context similar to many music programs.

Curriculum and Faculty

Identifying the quality of curriculum and teachers are steps necessary for program review. In reference to curriculum, varied and engaging program course offerings have a greater tendency to refine the instructional practices of teachers if a focus in program review is placed on evidence of student learning. In curriculum, offering a diverse set of courses can yield a broad range of data to document musical growth of students and the program across an array of musical learning. Furthermore, analysis of these data can expose areas where enhancement of content and instruction can improve learning. In respect to teaching, a well-defined and consistently administered student learning assessment process, evidence of ongoing instructional enhancement, and involvement in focused professional development can support claims of teacher quality.

Enrollment

Total contact time and enrollment are critical for most music educators in terms of program viability. More often than not, music educators focus on instrumentation and balance when considering enrollment needs and program health. Programs in many disciplines are often asked to meet enrollment needs to justify the use of district or state funds. Based on enrollment, directors can develop a recruiting strategy to address their needs as well as ensure sustained balance, learning growth, and musical development (Mitchell, Rudolph, Whitman, & Taylor, 1982; Sandene, 1994; Tracz, 1990; Byo, 1991).

While instrumentation and balance are important to performance ensembles, other documentation can provide valuable insights into a program's health. Other useful data include (a) interaction with past, current, and prospective students; (b) student-to-teacher ratio across the program analyzed across multiple years and projected into the future; (c) student attitudes and peer interaction; and (d) any other topic that can provide insight into a program's health. Establishing a system of assessments with a varied and robust protocol can be useful to understanding program heath.

Learning Experience:

(a) Enrollment data exercise: Use scenarios below to infer enrollment growth projections by instrument/voice category and grade level.

(b) Develop a recruiting strategy that includes a survey sent to current and prospective members intended to encourage growth.

Scenario #1	
District Information	
MS/HS Enrollment:	634
Choir Budget:	$ 1,500.00
Band Budget:	$ 3,000.00
Orchestra Budget:	$ 3,000.00
Choir Scenarios	
9-12 Enrollment	85
Mixed Choir	
Men	25
Women	55
Women's Choir	40
Show Choir	
Men	8
Women	10
Band Scenario	
6-12 Enrollment	157
HS	68
MS	89
Graduating	19
Low (< 4 in HS)	Clarinets
	Trombones
	Oboe
Orchestra Scenario	
6-12 Enrollment	124
HS	53
MS	71
Graduating	11
Low (< 4 in HS)	Viola

Scenario #2	
District Information	
Total MS/HS	
Enrollment:	256
Choir Budget:	$ 500.00
Band Budget:	$ 1,000.00
Orchestra	
Budget:	$ 1,000.00
Choir Scenarios	
9-12 Enrollment	54
Mixed Choir	
Men	14
Women	16
Beginning Choir	
Men	6
Women	18
Band Scenario	
9-12 Enrollment	36
Graduating	8
Low (< 4 in HS)	Flutes
	Tubas
Orchestra Scenario	
9-12 Enrollment	29
Graduating	4
Low (< 4 in HS)	Cello
	Viola

Community Connections

Identifying the needs of the local community and developing a plan for enhancing community connections are critical to a program's success and vitality. As a music educator, is it important to determine musical (or more broadly, the arts') needs of the community, connect with stakeholders in the region, and define the role of your program in your community. This will guide the decisions you make for your program, curriculum, and course development for the future years. This information can also be used to elicit funding sources and support beyond the traditional school budget. Yearly assessment of community relationships, connections, and needs can be a critical component of the program assessment process. One way to document contributions to the community is through feedback from performances held for and throughout the region. In addition to the aesthetic contribution to the community stakeholders, it is equally important to confirm the educational contribution of performances and musical experiences to student learning. Student learning has to be the foundational purpose of a school music program. Musical experiences, concerts, or other community engagements illustrate a bond between the community and the musical experience through which students learn. Strengthening emergent bonds over time requires sustained effort on the part of the music program teachers. Evidence of these efforts and its contribution to music learning will strengthen the viability, sustainability, and vibrancy of the program.

Learning Experience: Brainstorm the ways that a music class can contribute to the community. Then organize into the respective columns information that would be useful to guide program improvement and strategies to collect these data.

Ways to Contribute to the Community	Information That Can Be Gathered to Support Contribution	Strategies to Collect Data on Contribution

Student Learning Assessment Framework for a Program Review

In an era when meeting standards has become a determining factor of program success, establishing an assessment protocol that can demonstrate meeting of standards is critical. Outcome-based assessment is a process focused upon students attaining achievement levels of specified outcomes. Therefore, outcomes assessment comprises student-learning outcomes, curriculum intentionally designed to develop the intended learning, an assessment plan through which students demonstrate application of the outcomes, analysis of achievement data that differentiates levels of competence, data reporting to expose learning needs, and use of the findings to guide program improvement. Successful music programs excel when they define what they want their students to learn and how learning will be measured and use the data to meet students' learning needs.

Chapter 3 describes outcomes assessment using the 2014 National Standards for Music. The revised standards the three artistic processes: Create, Perform, and Respond, and 11 anchor standards are intended to guide program assessment in what the students "do" to demonstrate musical experience in music classes. They are useful to guide program review because they were developed across grade level and strands so as to embed assessments across a program and/or curriculum.

Detailed Assessment Process

Program effectiveness can be measured using a variety of techniques. A mixture of direct and indirect assessments should be employed to provide the information necessary to make informed decisions to guide decisions on program effectiveness. Student achievement data, stakeholder surveys, student surveys, current enrollment numbers, course offerings, and many more data points provide a balanced, holistic picture of a music program. These data are useful for sustaining a healthy and vibrant program and serve to provide context and meaning to the health, growth, and maintenance of a program for purposes of advocating to stakeholders or surrounding communities (see Opportunity to Learning Standards, 2015). Music program review should focus beyond maintenance and sustainability. It should identify the growth and development of its students and demonstrate success of the program completers (or graduates). The yearly data set should contain information that supports its claims of effectiveness. This information becomes a way to advocate for a music program, which includes documenting the musical growth and development of its students.

The Program Review Assessment Process

A program assessment process that focuses on student learning is foundational for a thorough program review. Learning goals, learning activities, and assessment protocols are essential considerations in an effective music program review (Fink, 2003). Program assessment confirms the extent to which music teachers utilize intentional student-learning outcomes to design instructional activities necessary to develop student proficiencies and the use of curriculum-integrated assessments that recognizes and differentiates levels of student achievement (Wiggins & McTighe, 2005). A comprehensive program assessment process often includes (a) establishment of program learning goals and student-learning outcomes; (b) the development of a curriculum map; (c) identification of data sets; (d) piloting, implementing, and collecting assessment data; and (e) data analysis and program improvements.

Program Goals

Establishing the purpose of your program through program learning goals is a critical step to uncover the situational factors surrounding your program (Fink, 2003). Program learning goals are often broad expectations of what students should be expected to know, do, and value as a result of being involved with your program (Gardiner, Corbitt, & Adams, 2009). These values should be further reflected in the curriculum structure, course-based strategies for teaching, and assessments of the learning quality (Fink, 2003; Wiggins & McTighe, 2005). The program goals should guide the focus of knowledge, skills, and dispositions within your school's educational context. An area often neglected in program review is the relevance of the program (and subject matter) in students' lives. It is important to focus all programmatic decision around how the program should evolve over time to reflect student needs and interests. Teacher introspection enables understanding of situational factors that interact with student learning. It is important to recognize what makes your music program relevant and challenging for your students. Program goals are intended to guide curriculum to develop creative, meaningful, and valued learning experiences.

Development of learning goals begins with an investigation of the student population, school and community expectations, curricular offerings, and expectations of the faculty. If there is a committee assigned to make assessment decisions, they all must understand the specific contexts in which the program must function. Some of the questions that will guide the development of your program goals are:

* Who are the students served by the program?
* What courses can be offered?
* How broad is the curriculum?
* How often does each course meet?
* What is the format of the daily/weekly schedule?
* What does the community expect from the music program?

Appraisals for these questions could come from a brief survey or a focus group with patrons, students, and stakeholders. Further guidance might come from other music faculty and district administrators. You and your colleagues must also reflect upon personal and professional expectations of the program and the district/state learning goals. Attention to the multiplicity of contextual factors is paramount to designing effective program reviews. Without consideration of situational factors, creating significant learning experiences for students and defining program success may be difficult.

Program review should confirm an intentional design of curriculum, course and content sequence, and course-based student learning objectives that are aligned with the mission of the program. An earlier chapter discussed the difference between program learning goals and course-level learning objectives. Contextual factors considered should be clearly evident in a program goals and learning objectives through the program review, such as contexts within the school district, external expectations of the local community and the musical community, nature of the courses offered in the curriculum, characteristics of the learners, characteristics of the faculty, and localized pedagogical challenges.

Learning Experience: Using the following Program Assessment Template, brainstorm the situational factors you feel could influence the quality of instruction and/or student learning experiences in a music program. Then explore the mechanisms that could be used to collect and explore data concerning these variables.

Situational Factors:	Enrollment: _____ Community expectations: _____ Learning expectations: _____ Student characteristics: _____ Existing challenges: _____		
Student Challenges that may result from the situational factors:	[Skills necessary to meet the stated objectives. Be as specific as possible]		
	Cognitive	Psychomotor	Affective
Program Goals:	[Ensuring a balance of knowledge, skills, and dispositions across domains.]		
Proposed Assessments:	[Minimum of 1 direct and 1 indirect assessment for each program goal.]		
Rationale:	[Describe how this plan will provide data needed to demonstrate meeting of the stated objectives.]		

Curriculum Map

An effective tool to document organization of student learning toward the program goals is a curriculum map (Jacobs, 2004). A curriculum map is an integral educational tool designed to sequence student learning across course offerings and identify opportunities for students to demonstrate learning through embedded assessments and guide instructional planning. The mapping process considers the what, when, and how and assessment processes designed to meet the stated learning goals (Harden, 2001). Sequencing students' experiences allows for effective development of learning within coursework that aligns with program goals (Uchiyama & Radin, 2009).

Learning Experience: List the learning necessary for the completion of an effective music program (learning goals). Then consider where across the curriculum learning development occurs within the sequence of courses. Using this information, create a curriculum map that will address the sequence of learning throughout a student's experience in your program.

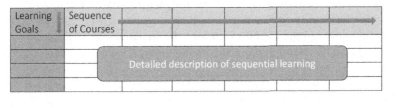

Assessment used for program review includes multiple measures used across the curriculum. As demonstrated on a curriculum map, achievement of student learning expected of program learning goals cannot be demonstrated by a single assessment. The curriculum map for your program should reflect the points of instruction for each learning goal, a clear sequence of development across courses, and a diagnostic component for quality control (Liu, Wrobbel, & Blankson, 2010). Payne, Burrack, Parkes, and Wesolowski (2019) suggest that embedding assessments across a curriculum will provide useful information to identify qualities of student learning so to guide instructional improvement. Embedded assessments, as well as developmental activities, when mapped across a program are used to document progressive musical development across a variety of activities and courses.

To guide the development of a curriculum map, it is important that you consider current music learning expectations of your local community as well as the regional culture. Studies have found that standards relevant to the educational context provide a strong framework for developing an effective assessment sequence (Moore & Kaplan, 2015). As discussed earlier in this chapter, the 2014 National Standards for Music and the aligned MCAs are a good starting point for mapping an effective student learning sequence (Burrack & Parkes, 2018). Their multi-year study on the development, piloting, and integration of MCAs established the reliability, validity, and fairness of the processes and scoring devices across multiple contexts. The MCAs and the accompanying text (Burrack & Parkes, 2018) are useful resources for designing or refining an assessment process for any music program.

Assessment Data

In program review, addressing the reliability, validity, and fairness of measures is vital to creating an effective assessment process (Payne et al., 2019). Consideration should also be given to timing of data collection, establishment of benchmark expectations, and integration of a feedback cycle to confirm usefulness. Part of this review should be deliberation as to when and how often students were provided feedback from formative assessments prior to the collection of summative achievement data used for program review. Development across day-to-day instruction prior to summative assessment is essential for effective documentation of student learning and the validity of the achievement scores. Balancing this process with class time and integration of assessments coursework is important so that the data reflect learning resulting from instruction. Earlier chapters addressed types of assessment formats, structures of assessment data, and issues of validity and reliability.

Establishing benchmarks for students at various points throughout the program is the component that ties assessments together in curriculum development. Identifying the quality of student learning expectations at various points across the program will enable the assessment measures to provide information appropriate for content, sequence, course offerings, etc. After several assessment cycles, trends of student achievement and learning needs will guide articulation pertaining to the effectiveness of the curriculum and instructional practice. It is not enough to look at enrollment numbers and course grades to establish program success.

Learning Experience: In small groups, brainstorm the various sources of data that could be useful to expose student-learning needs and to guide program improvement. For each data source:

- Identify the data needed.
- Develop a plan to collect the data.
- Create draft measures (forms, surveys, focus group questions, etc.).

Data Analysis and Program Improvements

One of the most vital parts of program review is often called closing the loop (Moore & Kaplan, 2015), which refers to using the collected data on the effectiveness to implement program improvements. Program review involves the measurement of a student's achievement over time for each of the program goals. Analysis of learning achieved and reflection of program goals is an important undertaking and a critical component of a program's assessment process. Outcome data must be analyzed to determine whether any actionable elements emerge. Identifying program success is an ultimate goal of program review, but an assessment process becomes useful when student learning challenges are exposed and the program initiates curricular and/or instructional revisions. The specificity of data that result from your assessment process enables you to reveal success as well as problems within a program, enabling you to address or remediate issues (Gardiner et al., 2009).

Once an annual program review is complete, program adjustments in instruction, content, and sequence might be necessary. This is when it is most important to convene with all faculty and stakeholders to discuss what the analyses revealed. For example, assessment analysis might reveal that content taught in a specific course might delay development in specific musical concepts as compared to content taught at a different place in the curricular sequence. Discussion that ensues could enable adjustment of the content sequence, ensuring the most effective sequence of instruction and course offerings. If discovered that students are progressing faster than expected, music selection and content difficulty could be adjusted to align with the enhanced student performance. Thoughtful analysis of student-learning outcomes can be in advocacy by demonstrating improvements made in your program.

Summary

Program assessment can take on the form of maintaining a set curriculum or specified output in terms of enrollment and program completers but should be designed to address the comprehensive nature of a music program including student learning. Enrollment, instrumentation, course offerings, student achievement, qualities of learning, community connections, and performances (local, regional, or national) should all be considered as essential factors in the complete narrative for program health. Identifying efficient and inefficient practices for data collection, documentation, student learning assessments, and reporting data is important in an effective program review. Used efficiently, program assessment can specifically address areas of strength and needs within a music program. If program assessment and annual program reviews become integrated within normal processes of music education, then program improvements can be consistent and supportive for a high-quality music program.

Activities and Worksheets

Class Activity 9.1: Advocate for Your Program

Your administration has just contacted you because the state has updated its curricular learning standards and the current curriculum is now outdated. Your charge is to research and develop an assessment plan that meets the state standards for your music program. Write a response to your superintendent reflecting your philosophy on the importance of student learning as the foundation of assessment, the process by which you will align your current curriculum with the new standards, an overview of your proposed curriculum structure reflected on a curriculum map, and ideas for creating an assessment plan.

Class Activity 9.2: State Your Case

You have just been informed that a revised grading policy is being implemented in your district. Participation grades will no longer be allowed as the primary source as program and course assessments. You are to find compelling cases in scholarly literature for performance assessment as well as developmental learning assessment. In groups, develop a case for why one should be considered over the other. Ground your argument in student learning and assessment. Present your findings as if you are presenting to the school board.

Class Activity 9.3: Program Assessment Revision

Your superintendent has just informed you that you will need to chair a committee to revise the district's music program assessment process. You are charged with developing a revised set of program goals, course offerings, and proposed assessments at the final board meeting of the year. Use the program assessment and curriculum map discussed earlier in this chapter to develop a presentation for your music teacher colleagues.

Class Activity 9.4: Assessment Portfolio

Your building principal has returned from an assessment conference and wants to perform an impromptu investigation of the assessment in your program. During the classroom visits and informal conversations, your administrator discovers that you have a strong foundation in assessment of student learning and asks that you make a short presentation to the faculty about your expertise in this area. One request is that an electronic handout be provided to your peers prior to the professional development session. The handout must contain the following sections:

1. Annotated list of eight assessments. Each annotation should include a definition and rationale for suggested uses in the music classroom.

2. Assessment matrix describing the administration and analysis of assessments across your program.
3. Outline of implementation for each assessment listed in Section 1. This outline should include a protocol for implementation in the classroom and a plan for establishing reliability and validity, as well as a process for analysis and subsequent adjustment.
4. Exemplar examples of each assessment in Section 1.

References

Burrack, F., & Parkes, K. (2018). *Applying Model Cornerstone Assessments in K-12 music: A research-supported approach*. New York: Rowman and Littlefield.

Byo, J. (1991). An assessment of musical instrument preferences of third-grade children. *Bulletin of the Council for Research in Music Education, 110*, 21–32.

Campbell, J., & Oblinger, D. (2007). Top-ten teaching and learning issues, 2007. *EDUCAUSE Quarterly, 30*(3), 15–22.

EDUCAUSE. (2019). *Key issues in teaching and learning*. [Online report from EDUCAUSE]. Retrieved from www.educause.edu/eli/initiatives/key-issues-in-teaching-and-learning

Fink, L. D. (2003). *Creating significant learning experiences*. San Francisco: Jossey-Bass.

Gardiner, L. R., Corbitt, G., & Adams, S. J. (2009). Program assessment: Getting to a practical how-to model. *Journal of Education for Business, 85*(3), 139–144. doi:10.1080/08832320903258576

Harden, R. M. (2001). AMEE guide no. 21: Curriculum mapping: A tool for transparent and authentic teaching and learning. *Medical Teacher, 23*, 123–137.

Jacobs, H. H. (Ed.). (2004). *Getting results with curriculum mapping*. Alexandria, VA: Association for Supervision and Curriculum Development.

Kokemuller, N. (2018). *Importance of mission vision in organizational strategy*. [Online blog post]. Retrieved February 13, 2019 from https://smallbusiness.chron.com/importance-mission-vision-organizational-strategy-16000.html

Liu, M., Wrobbel, D., & Blankson, I. (2010). Rethinking program assessment through the use of program alignment mapping technique. *Communication Teacher, 24*(4), 238–246. doi:10.1080/17404622.2010.513002

Mitchell, J. C., Rudolph, T. E., Whitman, T., & Taylor, J. A. (1982). Idea bank: Achieving balanced concert-band instrumentation. *Music Educators Journal, 68*(6), 40–41.

Moore, A. A., & Kaplan, J. J. (2015). Program assessment for an undergraduate statistics major. *The American Statistician, 69*(4), 1–32. doi:10.1080/0003130 5.2015.1087331

National Association for Music Education. (2015). *Opportunity to learning* standards. https://nafme.org/my-classroom/standards/opportunity-to-learn-standards/

Payne, P. D., Burrack, F., Parkes, K. A., & Wesolowski, B. (2019). An emerging process of assessment in music education. *Music Educators Journal, 105*(3), 36–44. https://doi.org/10.1177/0027432118818880

Sandene, B. A. (1994). Going beyond recruiting: Fighting attrition. *Music Educators' Journal, 81*(1), 32–34, 61.

Tracz, F. (1990). Winning the recruiting game. *The Instrumentalist, 45*(5), 84.
Uchiyama, K. P., & Radin, J. L. (2009). Curriculum mapping in higher education: A vehicle for collaboration. *Innovative Higher Education, 33,* 271–280.
Wiggins, G. P., & McTighe, J. (2005). *Understanding by design.* Alexandria, VA: Association for Supervision and Curriculum Development.

Glossary

Action verb The way students are expected to demonstrate learning.

Adaptation Students' abilities to transfer or modify technique to fit a specific situation (e.g., Students will be able to adapt, rearrange, revise, vary).

Affective domain The manner in which students develop in areas such as feelings, values, appreciation, enthusiasms, motivations, and attitudes.

Analyze (skill) Students' abilities to break down communication into its constituent elements or parts such that the relative hierarchy of ideas is made clear and/or the relations between ideas expressed are made explicit (e.g., Students will be able to differentiate, outline, relate).

Anchor standards The general knowledge and skill that educators expect students to demonstrate throughout their education in the arts (National Core Arts Music Standards, 2014).

Application (apply) Students' abilities to use abstractions in particular and concrete situations (e.g., Students will be able to classify, graph, modify); to apply knowledge or skills to new situations, use information and knowledge to solve a problem, answer a question, or perform another task (e.g., Students will be able to classify, graph, modify).

Artistic processes The cognitive and physical actions by which arts learning and making are realized (National Core Arts Music Standards, 2014).

Assessment (process) The collection, analysis, interpretation, and applied response to information about student performance or program effectiveness in order to make educational decisions resulting in continual improvement.

Assessment blueprint A concise plan of action that captures the multiple methods in which an educator intends to formally test students' academic performance in the classroom within a given instructional unit.

Assessment task Activity or test designed to measure and evaluate a student's demonstration of attained knowledge, specific skills, or expected dispositions.

Authentic assessment   An assessment task that reflects the way a student thinks and interacts in an authentic environment connecting with belief and experiences within each individual student.

Benchmark   A standard or point of reference against which things may be compared or evaluated.

Characterization   Students' abilities to establish a value system that informs their behaviors and decision-making (e.g., displays, modifies, solves). Also see valuing.

Cognitive domain   Mental skills and acquisition of knowledge.

Complex overt response   Students' efficiency of technique (same as mechanism, but students demonstrate more efficiency and faster speed).

Comprehension   Students' abilities to understand such that they know what is being communicated and can make use of the material or idea being communicated without necessarily relating it to other material or seeing its fullest implications (e.g., Students will be able to associate, explain, generalize).

Communication of expectations   The teacher ensures that the student has a comprehensive understanding of the teacher's learning outcome expectations.

Conditions   The situation or context of the learners.

Congruency   The relationship of the outcome of the test with previous patterns of student achievement.

Construct validity   How well the items function together to represent the construct being measured.

Content standards   Collections of statements that describe specific desired learning outcomes or objectives.

Content validity   How adequately the content of the test covers the construct being measured.

Create   Students' abilities to pull together parts of knowledge to form a new whole and build relationships for new situations (e.g., Students will be able to generate, reconstruct, rewrite).

Criteria types   The evaluative criteria included in a checklist, rating scale, or rubric.

Criterion   A defined expectation of the standard of performance for a particular task (plural: criteria).

Criterion validity   The extent to which a test matches related outcomes of a similar test measuring the same construct.

Criterion-referenced tests   Tests used to measure students' achievement against predetermined criteria or standards of learning.

Data   A set of collected information, either words or numbers.

Dichotomous   When test responses require either a correct or incorrect response.

Differentiation of assessment types   The use of multiple assessment types to ensure a student's opportunity to demonstrate student-learning outcomes.

Direct assessment   An assessment that measures an observable demonstration of learning.

Dispositions   A person's inherent or developed habits of mind and character.

Documentation   The method used to record student achievement through scores and illustrative examples for evaluation and accountability.

Educational assessment   The methods and tools used for documenting and evaluating student knowledge, skill, and disposition to make educational decisions for teaching and learning.

Educational taxonomies   Levels of learning taking place within the classroom.

Enduring understandings   Statements summarizing the important ideas and core processes that are central to a discipline and having lasting value beyond the classroom (National Core Arts Music Standards, 2014).

Essential questions   Questions that lie at the heart of a subject or a curriculum and promote inquiry and ultimately an emergence of a subject (National Core Arts Music Standards, 2014).

Evaluation (process)   The collection and analysis of assessment data to make decisions about student achievement or program effectiveness, making informed educational decisions.

Evaluation (skill)   Students' judgments about the value of material and methods for given purposes (e.g., Students will be able to contrast, grade, rank).

Exemplar   A person or thing serving as an excellent model.

Fairness   Responsiveness to individual characteristics and testing contexts so that test scores will yield valid interpretations for intended uses.

Formative assessment   Ongoing assessment within an educational program for the purpose of exposing learning needs and guiding improvements.

Grading   The assignment of value to that performance or growth demonstrated.

Guided response   Related to rote learning and guided practice, students copy, reproduce, or respond.

Illustrative example   Student work that serves as a model for meeting a specific set of criteria.

Inferences   The conclusions that are made by the teacher about the adequacy of the test in regard to the latent construct being measured, the data-gathering procedures, the level of achievement of the student, and their interpretation of the data gathered from the test.

Item difficulty indices   An index for exploring the proportion of students who answered an item correctly and incorrectly.

Item-discrimination indices   An important index for empirically exploring the quality of the response patterns of the items.

Item functioning A statistical characteristic of an item that shows the extent to which the item might be measuring different abilities for members of separate subgroups.

Item-types The type of items used to capture the student behavior (e.g., multiple choice, fill-in-the-blank, short answer).

Item response theory (IRT) The psychometric model that focuses on the properties of each item (question) in a test. IRT can explain relationships between latent traits (characteristics or attributes that are not observable) and the observed outcomes, responses, or performances.

Knowledge level Students' abilities to recall specifics and universals; methods and processes; or patterns, structures, or settings (e.g., Students will be able to recognize, recall, identify).

Latent constructs Any construct that cannot be directly measured but rather inferred through the measurement of secondary behaviors.

Learning Management System A software application for the administration, documentation, tracking, reporting, and delivery of educational courses or training programs.

Learning objective Statements that define the expected learning in a course, lesson, or activity in terms of demonstrable skills or knowledge that will be acquired by a student as a result of instruction.

Learning outcome Statements that describe significant and essential learning that students have achieved and can reliably demonstrate at the end of a course or program. In other words, what the learner will know and be able to do by the end of a course or program.

Level A descriptor that describes the knowledge, skill, and/or disposition performance level of students to allow teachers to determine an achievement score.

Level of thinking processes The considerations of the cognitive rigor of the test in relation to the cognitive rigor of the course content and student abilities.

Measurement The use of systematic methodology to quantify musical behaviors in order to represent the magnitude of performance capability, task completion, and concept attainment.

Mechanism level Students' development of performance habits (e.g., Students will be able to fix, manipulate, organize, sketch).

Mission statement A formal summary of the aims and values of an academic program or organization.

Model Cornerstone Assessments (MCAs) Curriculum-embedded assessment tasks and measures designed for music students to apply developmentally appropriate and relevant knowledge and skills while demonstrating learning defined in standards.

Norm-referenced testing Testing in which students' test scores are compared against the local, district, state, or national average scores of other students of the same age/grade level.

Organization   Students' priority of values through comparing and synthesis (e.g., compares, relates, synthesizes).

Origination level   The origination level includes the students' abilities to establish new techniques to make current study more efficient (e.g., Students will be able to arrange, compose, create).

Perception   When students use sensory clues to guide motor activity (e.g., Students will be able to choose, describe, detect, isolate).

Performance assessment   An assessment that requires students to demonstrate learning by integrating expected knowledge, skills, and/or dispositions; the learning goal is assessed via a performance task (but is not limited to only musical performances) and a defined scoring guide or rubric.

Performance standards   Described level of performance required for a test taker to be classified into a given performance quality.

Person ability indices   An important index for exploring the proportion of items that were answered correctly or incorrectly by an individual student.

Person-discrimination indices   An important index for empirically exploring the quality of the response patterns of the individual students.

Person functioning   A statistical characteristic of an item that shows the extent to which the item might be measuring individual student-centered behaviors of engagement with the test.

Polytomous   Items that have more than two possible scores.

Portfolio assessment   An analysis of a collection of student work used to demonstrate student achievement in a content area; student progress is determined by reviewing the collected works in light of previously established criteria.

Process components   The actions artists carry out as they complete each artistic process (National Core Arts Music Standards, 2014).

Program assessment   The systematic and ongoing method of gathering, analyzing, and using information from various sources about a program and measuring program outcomes in order to improve the quality of the program and student learning.

Program goals   General statements of what the program intends to accomplish.

Program learning goals   General statements of what the program intends for students to learn, what skills they develop, and what experiences they will have (or likely have) as a result of completing the requirements for the program.

Program review   A rigorous, systematic, objective, impartial, expert-based examination, evaluation, and self-evaluation of how effectively a program is working, as part of the ongoing pursuit of higher levels of achievement in the service of program improvement.

Psychomotor domain   Physical movement, coordination, and the use of fine motor skills.

Receiving   Students' awareness of surrounding stimuli and observants (e.g., acknowledge, listen, be attentive).

Relevance   The alignment between the content of the test and any related national/state standards and learning objectives that underscore the related teaching.

Remember (recall)   Students' abilities to recall information such as dates, events, places, ideas, definitions, or theories (e.g., Students will be able to recognize, recall, identify).

Reliability   The consistency of an assessment task or tool to produce similar results over a given amount of time. In a classroom setting, dependability of the test to adequately support the inferences made about the student-learning outcomes.

Responding   Students' attention and specific reactions to given stimuli (e.g., assists, conforms, presents).

Responsiveness   The ability of a measure to change over a pre-specified time frame and the extent to which change in a measure relates to corresponding change in a reference.

Rubric   A set of scoring criteria used to determine the value of a student's performance on assigned tasks; the criteria are written so students are able to learn what must be done to improve their performances in the future.

Scoring device(s)   The type of instrument used to collect evidence of student behaviors, including but not limited to checklists, rating scales, criteria-specific rating scales, rubrics, multiple-choice items, matching items, essays, and matching tests.

Self-assessment   Analysis of one's own knowledge, skills, and dispositions.

Standard   The content, level, or type of performance expected of students at a particular point in time or stage of development

Standardize   To cause an assessment to conform to a standard.

Standards-aligned   A system of instruction, assessment, and documentation focused on students' demonstration of knowledge, skills, and dispositions to a mutually agreed upon set of intended student-learning outcomes or expectations as they progress through their education.

Student opportunities   The ability of the student to adequately and accurately demonstrate their ability to meet student-learning outcomes in varied ways.

Summative assessment   An assessment at the end of an instruction cycle to measure student growth and learning.

Synthesis   Students' abilities to put together elements and parts so as to form a whole (e.g., Students will be able to generate, reconstruct, rewrite).

Systematic assessment procedures   The teacher ensuring student understanding, familiarity, and engagement with assessment procedures.

Table of specifications   A two-dimensional matrix that describes the content, structure, and learning outcomes of a specific assessment instrument.

Test   In the context of a music classroom, any circumstance in which a teacher makes a systematic observation of students' musical behavior.

Transparency   The clear communication between teacher and student in regard to the testing context, testing content, and testing use.

Understanding   Students' abilities to grasp meaning of the information, express it in their own words, and cite examples (e.g., Students will be able to associate, explain, generalize).

Validity   The effectiveness of an assessment instrument in measuring what it is supposed to measure; also the appropriate use of assessment data in reporting and analysis.

Valuing   Students attach to a specific entity, object, or experience (e.g., appreciates, justifies, respects).

*All definitions were synthesized from multiple sources by the authors.

About the Authors

Frederick Burrack, Ph.D., is Director of Assessment, Professor of Music Education, Graduate Chair for Music, Distinguished Graduate Faculty. He has served as the Chair for the National Association for Music Education Assessment Special Research Interest Group and as Co-Chair for their work in developing Model Cornerstone Assessments that accompany the National K-12 Music Standards. His co-edited book *Applying Model Cornerstone Assessments in K–12 Music: A Research-Supported Approach* was published in 2018.

Kelly A. Parkes, Ph.D., is Director and Associate Professor of the Music and Music Education at Teachers College, Columbia University. She directs the Teacher Certification program for pre-service teachers in Music and is the Chair of the Teacher Education Policy Committee. Her research agenda is focused in assessment of teaching and learning in the applied studio in higher education and in K-12 schools, in motivation/efficacy, in pedagogical technology, and in music teacher education. She served on the team that produced the NAfME (2013, 2016) *Workbooks for Building and Evaluating Music Education* and currently serves on the editorial review committee of the *Journal of Research in Music Education*.

Phillip Payne, Ph.D., is an Associate Professor of Music Education at Kansas State University. He teaches undergraduate and graduate classes in music education and supervises student teachers. He maintains an active research agenda as well as serving as an adjudicator, clinician, and guest conductor throughout the Midwestern United States.

Brian C. Wesolowski, Ph.D., is an Associate Professor of Music Education at the University of Georgia, Hugh Hodgson School of Music. His primary research interest includes the study of rater behavior, scale development, the policy of educational assessment, and broad applications of assessment, measurement, and evaluation in large-scale testing and classroom contexts.

Index

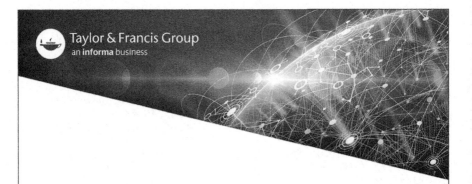

Made in the USA
Las Vegas, NV
02 May 2022

48326509R00118